"Apart from Freud's classic case-studies, Lacan discussed relatively few clinical cases in his seminars and written texts. The one major exception to this rule is the case of the man who came to be known as 'fresh-brains man', who had the unusual privilege of becoming the subject of psychoanalytic reflection in published papers by each of the two psychoanalysts he had consulted. In this meticulously researched, tightly argued, and conceptually accessible book, Benvenuto not only surveys Lacan's numerous interpretations of the analyses of 'fresh-brains man', but also points out some of his debatable comments and his own puzzling (mis)readings of the case. This truly terrific study will not only be extremely valuable to all Lacan scholars, but appeal to every clinician and researcher who is interested in the question of psychoanalytic technique and the enduring richness of historical cases."

—**Professor Dany Nobus**, *Brunel University, London*

"Who would wish to pick a psychoanalyst's brain? Dissecting the case of Professor 'Brain' as approached by two major psychoanalysts, Ernst Kris, who treated the analysand, and Jacques Lacan, who contradictorily revisited it on several occasions, Sergio Benvenuto unravels psychoanalytic criticism, sheds new light on the analytic process itself, and delves into the complexities of the analyst's desire. Benvenuto's detailed deconstructive study is written with humor and accessible erudition, offering a stimulating read as well as an exploration of the challenges of transmission."

—**Patricia Gherovici**, *psychoanalyst and author of* Transgender Psychoanalysis: A Lacanian Perspective on Sexual Difference

"Like a veteran seafarer charting a vessel through contested waters, Benvenuto dedicates himself to the precise task of untying knots. True to his inimitable style, Benvenuto's deconstructions bring a fierce, clarifying light to long-held entanglements, oversights, and prejudices, helping to draw new, vitalizing blood from a whole host of analytic artefacts. Much is to be learned from this delightful text, not only in terms of the materials at hand, but the manner in which the author works with them. Equal parts philosopher, historian, social scientist, and psychoanalyst, Benvenuto's synthesizing style allows us to sail forth, transmitting the essentials of psychoanalytic practice and thought to present and future generations."

—**Fernando Castrillon, Psy.D.**, *personal and supervising psychoanalyst, editor-in-chief*, European Journal of Psychoanalysis

Lacan, Kris and the Psychoanalytic Legacy: The Brain Eater

Lacan, Kris and the Psychoanalytic Legacy: The Brain Eater examines the case of a scholar which was commented on by three leading psychoanalysts of the 20th century: Melitta Schmideberg, Ernst Kris, and Jacques Lacan.

Sergio Benvenuto unpicks the complex case history of the patient he calls "Professor Brain", a man who struggled to publish his research because of his fixation on plagiarism and who has never been identified. Benvenuto reconstructs the case through the first-hand accounts of the patient's analysts and Lacan and sets it in the context of mid-century psychoanalytic debate. As we progress through the patient's story, Benvenuto explains Lacan's theories as they apply to the case: the "foreclosure" of orality; obsessional neurosis; mental anorexia; and, above all, the reasons for his opposition to Ego psychology, of which Kris was one of the most important representatives.

This book will be of great interest to psychoanalysts in practice and in training, psychiatrists and clinical psychologists. It will also be of interest to academics and scholars of philosophy, the history of psychoanalysis, literature and cultural studies.

Sergio Benvenuto is a psychoanalyst in Rome, president of the Institute for Advanced Studies in Psychoanalysis and founder and former editor of the European Journal of Psychoanalysis. He is a member of the Institute of Sciences and Technologies of Cognition at the Italian Council for Scientific Research.

Lacan, Kris and the Psychoanalytic Legacy

The Brain Eater

Sergio Benvenuto

R Routledge
Taylor & Francis Group

LONDON AND NEW YORK

Designed cover image: © Getty Image

First published 2024
by Routledge
4 Park Square, Milton Park, Abingdon, Oxon OX14 4RN

and by Routledge
605 Third Avenue, New York, NY 10158

Routledge is an imprint of the Taylor & Francis Group, an informa business

British Library Cataloguing-in-Publication Data
A catalogue record for this book is available from the British Library

Library of Congress Cataloging-in-Publication Data
Names: Benvenuto, Sergio, author.
Title: Lacan, Kris and the psychoanalytic legacy : the brain eater /
    Sergio Benvenuto.
Description: Abingdon, Oxon ; New York, NY : Routledge, 2024. |
    Includes bibliographical references and index.
Identifiers: LCCN 2023010802 (print) | LCCN 2023010803 (ebook) |
    ISBN 9781032482354 (hardback) | ISBN 9781032482330 (paperback) |
    ISBN 9781003388098 (ebook)
Subjects: LCSH: Lacan, Jacques, 1901–1981. | Kris, Ernst, 1900–1957. |
    Psychoanalysis—Case studies. | Psychotherapy—Case studies.
Classification: LCC BF173.L15 B464 2024 (print) | LCC BF173.L15
    (ebook) | DDC 150.19/509—dc23/eng/20230602
LC record available at https://lccn.loc.gov/2023010802
LC ebook record available at https://lccn.loc.gov/2023010803

ISBN: 978-1-032-48235-4 (hbk)
ISBN: 978-1-032-48233-0 (pbk)
ISBN: 978-1-003-38809-8 (ebk)

DOI: 10.4324/9781003388098

Typeset in Times New Roman
by Apex CoVantage, LLC

Contents

Abbreviations

Works of Sigmund Freud
SE The Standard Edition of the Complete Psychological Works of Sigmund Freud,
    The Hogarth Press and the Institute of Psycho-analysis, London.
GW Gesammelte Werke, Fischer Taschenbuch Verlag, Frankfurt Am Main.
Works of Jacques Lacan
E I Écrits I, Éditions du Seuil, Paris 1999.
E II Écrits II, Éditions du Seuil, Paris 1999.
Écrits The First Complete Edition in English. Eng. trans. by Bruce Fink in collabo-
    ration with Héloïse Fink and Russell Grigg, Norton, New York 2002.
Aut. E. Autres écrits, Éditions du Seuil, Paris 2001.
Se1 Le Séminaire, livre 1. Les écrits techniques de Freud, Éditions du Seuil, Paris
    1975.
Sem 1 Freud's Papers on Technique: The Seminar of Jacques Lacan, Book I (1953–
    1954). Edited by Jacques-Alain Miller. Eng. trans. by John Forrester, Norton,
    New York, 1988.
Se3 Le Séminaire, livre 3. Les psychoses, Éditions du Seuil, Paris 1981.
Sem 3 The Psychoses: The Seminar of Jacques Lacan, Book III (1955–1956). Ed-
    ited by Jacques-Alain Miller. Eng. trans. by Russell Grigg, Norton, New York,
    1997.
Se4 Le Séminaire, livre 4. La relation d'objet, Éditions du Seuil, Paris 1994.
Sem 4 The Object Relation: The Seminar of Jacques Lacan, Book IV (1956–1957).
    Edited by Jacques-Alain Miller. Eng. trans. by A. R. Price, Polity, Cambridge, 2021.
Se5 Le Séminaire, livre 5. Les formations de l'inconscient, Éditions du Seuil, Paris 1998.
Sem 5 The Formations of the Unconscious: The Seminar of Jacques Lacan, Book
    V (1957–1958). Edited by Jacques-Alain Miller. Eng. trans. by Russell Grigg,
    Polity, Cambridge, 2017.
Se6 Le Séminaire, livre 6. Le désir et son interprétation, Editions du Seuil, Paris
    2013.
Sem 6 Desire and its Interpretation: The Seminar of Jacques Lacan, Book VI
    (1958–1959). Edited by Jacques-Alain Miller. Eng. trans. by Bruce Fink, Polity,
    Cambridge, 2019.
Se7 Le Séminaire, livre 7. L'éthique de la psychanalyse, Éditions du Seuil, Paris
    1986.

Sem 7 The Ethics of Psychoanalysis: The Seminar of Jacques Lacan, Book VII (1959–1960). Edited by Jacques-Alain Miller. Eng. trans. by Dennis Porter, Norton, New York, 1992.

Se8 Le Séminaire, livre 8. Le transfert, Éditions du Seuil, Paris 1991.

Sem 8 Transference: The Seminar of Jacques Lacan, Book VIII (1960–1961). Edited by Jacques-Alain Miller. Eng. trans. by Bruce Fink, Polity, Cambridge, 2015.

Se10 Le Séminaire, livre 10. L'angoisse, Editions du Seuil, Paris 2004.

Sem 10 Anxiety: The Seminar of Jacques Lacan, Book X (1962–1963). Edited by Jacques-Alain Miller. Eng. trans. by A. R. Price, Polity, Cambridge, 2014.

Se20 Le Séminaire, livre 20. Encore, Éditions du Seuil, Paris, 1975.

Sem 20 Encore, On Feminine Sexuality, the Limits of Love and Knowledge: The Seminar of Jacques Lacan, Book XX (1972–1973). Edited by Jacques-Alain Miller. Eng. trans. by Bruce Fink, Norton, New York, 1998.

Se23 Le Séminaire, livre 23, Le sinthome, Editions du Seuil, Paris 2005.

In this book, when I quote from the English edition of Lacan's works, I have sometimes slightly modified the translation from the French.

Acknowledgements

This book saw the light of day in a first Italian edition thanks to Federico Leoni of the University of Padua, who included it in the Orthotes publishing house series that he edited.

I found support and encouragement in friends like Alessandra Campo, Cristiana Cimino and Patrizia Crippa, as well as in my impartial (and strict) editorial judge Renato Benvenuto. I wish to thank Matteo Bonazzi, Raffaele Bracalenti and Arturo Casoni for organizing public discussions on my book.

For the English version, I wish thank Fernando Castrillón for his valuable advice and publishing contacts. This English edition, expanded compared to the original, is thanks to the rescuing help of my nephew Gianmaria Senia and of Emma Gainsforth and thanks to Agnès Jacob's and Chloe Chard's re-readings of the entire text. A very special thanks to Patricia Gherovici. And above all, thanks to the support, linguistic, too, of my life partner Claudia Vaughn, thanks to whom I am what I am.

Commenting on a Text Is Like Conducting an Analysis

Lacan (*Sem 1*, 73)

The character discussed in this book has no name. He was the patient of two analysts, and they could not reveal it. So I shall give him a fictional name: Professor Brain.

The case of Professor Brain has had the privilege of being described and commented upon in works by three eminent analysts in three different languages: in German by his first analyst, Melitta Schmideberg (1934); in English by his second analyst, Ernst Kris (1948);[1] and in French, seven times between 1954 and 1967, by Jacques Lacan,[2] a sign that analysts found this gentleman's story especially intriguing. I am in fact surprised that no historian has ever considered investigating who this person really was, as was done systematically for all of Freud's cases.

Notes

1 The case was presented in December 1948 to the panel on Technical Implications of Ego Psychology of the American Psychoanalytic Association, published in Kris (1951) and republished in Kris (1953). In this book the quotes from Kris's text are taken from the first edition of 1951.
2 *Sem 1*, 59–61, 10 February 1954; *Sem 2*, 79–81, 11 January 1956; "Response to Jean Hyppolite's Commentary on Freud's 'Verneinung'", March 1956, in *Écrits*, 318–333; "The Direction of the Treatment and the Principles of Its Power", 13 July 1958, published in 1961, later in *Écrits*, 489–542; *Sem 6*, 482, 1 July 1959; *Sem 10* 124, 23 January 1963; *La logique du fantasme: Séminaire 1966–1967*, session of 8 March 1967 (Association Lacanienne Internationale, 2004).

Chapter 1

Lacan and Kris's Plagiarist

Here we shall proceed with the text by Lacan, who did not have him as one of his *analysands* – like Lacan, this is what we shall call those who are still commonly referred to as patients of analysts – but who refers to him in his discussions of Kris's text. He discusses the case for the first time on 10 February 1954, in his seminar.

> I promised you another example, which I am taking from the advocates of the so-called modern way of analysing. You'll see that these principles were already set out in 1925 in this text of Freud's.[1]
>
> A great deal is made of the fact that at first we analyse the surface, as they say. It would be the crowning glory to make it possible for the subject to progress by escaping this sort of chance represented by the intellectualized sterilisation of contents re-evoked by analysis.
>
> Well, Kris, in one of his articles, gives an account of the case of a subject whom he took into analysis and who, it should be said, had already been analysed once. This subject is seriously hampered in his profession, an intellectual profession which appears to be, in the glimpses one catches of it, not far removed from what might be our preoccupations. This subject experiences all manner of difficulties producing, as they say. Indeed, his life is as it were fettered by the feeling he has of being, let's say for the sake of brevity, a plagiarist. He is continually discussing his ideas with someone very close to him, a brilliant *scholar*, but he always feels tempted to take on the ideas his interlocutor provides him with, and that is for him a perpetual impediment to everything that he wants to get out, to publish.
>
> All the same, he manages to get one text into shape. But, one day, he turns up declaring almost triumphantly that the whole of his thesis is already to be found in the library, in a published article. So there he is, this time, a plagiarist despite himself.
>
> What will the alleged interpretation of the surface that Kris offers us actually consist in? Probably in the following – Kris in actual fact becomes interested in what happened and what the article contains. Looking into it more closely, he realises that none of the central theses brought forward by the subject are to be found there. Some issues are raised which address the same question, but there

DOI: 10.4324/9781003388098-1

is nothing of the new views brought forward by his patient, whose thesis is thus clearly original. This is where you must start, Kris says, it's what he calls – I don't know why – taking up things on the surface.

Now, Kris says, if the subject is bent on showing him that his entire behaviour is completely shackled, it is because his father never succeeded in producing anything, because he was crushed by a *grand-père* [grandfather; literally: a great father] – in all the senses of the word – who himself had a highly constructive and fertile mind. He needs to find in his father a grand-father, a really great father who, in contrast, would be capable of achieving something, and he satisfies this need by forging himself tutors, always greater than him, upon whom he becomes dependent by means of a plagiarism for which he then reproaches himself and by means of which he destroys himself. He is thus doing nothing more than satisfying a need, the same need that tormented his childhood and, as a consequence, dominated his history.

There is no question it is a valid interpretation. And it is important to see how the subject reacted to it. What does Kris consider the confirmation of the significance of what he put forward, and which goes such a long way?

In what follows we see the whole history of the subject unfolding. We see that the symbolisation, properly speaking penile, of this need for the real, creative and powerful, father, took the form of all sorts of games in childhood, fishing games – will the father catch a bigger or a smaller fish? etc. But the immediate reaction of the subject is the following. He remains silent, and at the following session he says – *The other day, on leaving, I walked on such and such a street –* it takes place in New York, it is the street where there are foreign restaurants where you can eat rather spicier dishes [*re-levés*] – *and I looked for a place where I could find the dish I am particularly fond of, fresh brains.*

Here you can see what makes for a response elicited by an accurate interpretation, namely a level of speech which is both paradoxical and full in its meaning.

What makes this an accurate interpretation? Are we dealing with something which is at the surface? What does that mean? It means nothing other than that Kris, via a detour that is doubtless diligent, but whose outcome he could easily have predicted, came to realise precisely the following – that the subject, in his manifestation in this special guise of the production of an organised discourse, in which he is always subject to this process which is called negation [*dénégation*] and in which the integration of his ego is accomplished, can only reflect his fundamental relation to his ideal ego in an inverted form.

In other words, the relation to the other, in so far as the primitive desire of the subject strives to manifest itself in it, always contains in itself this fundamental, original element of negation, which here takes the form of inversion.

(*Se1*, pp. 71–72. *Sem 1*, pp. 59–61)

Note

1 Here Lacan refers to Freud's "Die Verneinung" ("Negation", S. Freud, 1925) previously commented upon by Jean Hyppolite.

Chapter 2

The Plagiarized Plagiarist

As we can see, Lacan's commentary consists essentially of praise – "There is no question it is a valid interpretation", he says. Yet he would completely reverse this benevolent attitude when he took up the same case in 1956 (in *Seminar 3* and in an essay), again in 1958 and later: on these occasions he attacked Kris violently, ridiculing him. Here he limits himself to disputing the expression "taking up things on the surface", which he claims not to understand. But now I would like to focus above all on the various discrepancies between Lacan's account and Kris's original text.

We shall point them out – let me make it immediately clear – not because my aim is to discredit Lacan's commentary or imply that he was in bad faith. Besides, Kris's text was published in a widely available journal, and anyone would have been able to spot the discrepancies, which could even depend on Lacan's imperfect fluency in English. Lacan himself had invited his pupils to read the text by Kris. We shall treat them as *misunderstandings*, a dimension psychoanalysis has rarely investigated, though closely related to the slip of the tongue. (Heidegger, 1967,[1] considered *misunderstanding*, together with *idle talk* and *curiosity*, one of the typical forms of inauthentic existence.) Misinterpreting a text, seeing something in it that it does not contain, or not seeing what it does contain, is a form of lapsus that the subject does not recognize as such. It is, let's say, *a slip according to the other* (and those who misinterpret often deny having done so). It should in any case attract analytic interpretation. It is from these slips-misunderstandings of Lacan's that we shall try, following the unpaved road of psychoanalysis, to understand what Lacan really tried to say, perhaps without being fully aware of it himself.

First of all, Kris's text does not in any way mention a subsequent session. He writes "the patient was silent. . . . Then, as if reporting a sudden insight, he said . . .". The whole issue – Kris's interpretation and the account of the culinary adventure – takes place in the same session. Why does Lacan introduce this discontinuity between sessions? At any rate, in the 1956 text, in which he takes up the case again, this reference to a succession of sessions is no longer present. Lacan had obviously read Kris's text again. In the seminar he spoke off the cuff, so he could distort many details. But psychoanalysis itself helps us see the sheer significance of the distortions that memory imprints on experience.

DOI: 10.4324/9781003388098-2

The explanation for this discrepancy will appear as closely linked to another discrepancy. Lacan, quoting the patient, says: "The other day I walked on such and such a street –", implying that Brain went out in search of fresh brains after being given Kris's interpretation. But Kris had Brain say: "Every noon, when I leave here, before luncheon . . . I walk through X Street". It wasn't something Brain had done once but something he'd been doing habitually for some time at the end of every session with Kris. As we shall see, it is this infidelity to the text that will allow Lacan, sometime later, to interpret this search for fresh brains as an acting out.

According to Lacan, the street where Mr. Brain looked for fresh brains was one "where you can have spicier food" ("*l'on mange des choses un peu relevées*"; *relevées* means refined, spicy, well-seasoned). But Kris only wrote "I walk through X Street [a street well known for its small but attractive restaurants] and I look at the menus in the windows". He speaks of "small but attractive restaurants" without mentioning in any way that they were foreign or that they served spicy or refined dishes. In addition, fresh brains are a dish, not a *repas*, a meal, as Lacan says. What leads Lacan to imagining this setting of exotic restaurants with spicy or unusual foods, refined establishments where – as he wrote in 1956 – "*l'on est bien soigné*", where customers are apparently treated in a special way?[2] Why did Lacan see this whole Hollywood movie scenario in the simple expression "*attractive restaurants*"? Was it a gimmick to captivate his audience, tired after some two hours of seminar? Kris's text – like ultimately any text – functions here as a Rorschach inkblot, so Lacan "sees" in it his own phantasms. "Fresh brains" clearly evoke in Lacan a *reverie*, as Bion would say, an entire universe of shady Asian restaurants, possibly in Manhattan's Chinatown, of perverted meals based on brains, maybe with young prostitutes ready to enjoy a spice-laden meal. . . . Rather than lost in translation, here much is enriched in translation.

Above all, however, a quick fact-check rules out the possibility that Prof. Brain lived in New York. We can say with certainty that his analysis took place in London.[3] In fact, in a note, Kris tells us that the analysis with Brain was interrupted by the outbreak of World War II and wonders why. Perhaps the patient was called up for active service or could no longer see Kris because Kris moved to the United States in 1940? Kris lived in the English capital between 1938 and 1940. In 1938, after Hitler's *Anschluss* of Austria, Kris left Vienna for London, where he stayed for around two years before moving to New York in 1940 to escape the war. In London Kris began an analysis with Anna Freud, and his flight to the United States caused him to interrupt it.

Lacan knew that Prof. Brain had already been analysed, years earlier, by Melitta Schmideberg-Klein, daughter of Melanie Klein, who discussed this case in an essay published in 1934, when she was living not in New York but in London. She'd moved to the English capital with her mother sometime between 1928 and 1930 and lived there until 1945, when Melitta moved to New York with her husband, eleven years after the case was published. Both of Prof. Brain's analyses, therefore, took place in London. Unless it was Brain who moved from London to New York in the course of the war. . . . But Kris tells us that it was the war that separated them, and I don't believe that even if his patient, a Briton, had emigrated to the United States, he would have been drafted there!

I would also like to venture a hypothesis: that Prof. Brain, although pursuing a career in England, was German speaking. Can we then assume that Prof. Brain was a Berliner, since Schmideberg lived in Berlin more or less from 1928 to 1931? Can we also assume that Prof. Brain was Jewish and that he left Germany for Britain in 1933 with the advent of Hitler? That is, Berlin and London would then be the cities of his two analyses. But this hypothesis is unlikely, since Kris speaks of him as a young man in his early thirties. If he was 32 in 1938, at what age would he have undergone his first analysis with Schmideberg in Berlin? At 25? But Schmideberg already describes him as someone actively engaged in scientific work (see the quotation from Schmideberg subsequently), not as a student.

I cannot say what Kris's level of English was in 1938 when he'd just landed in England, nor do I know what Schmideberg's English was like when she analysed the patient in the early 1930s. But the fact that he chose two German-speaking analysts who had recently left their country and moved to London might lead us to suspect that Professor Brain was a German speaker himself. This is not the essential point.

What inspired Lacan to see a New Yorker in a scholar who was actually based in England? It is true that in his 1956 text Lacan no longer says that the city in which the story takes place is New York (in the meantime he must have thought it over, perhaps on similar grounds to those suggested here), but the continual, repeated references to Americanism – in 1956, he even makes an ironic reference to Roosevelt's New Deal, comparing it to the *new deal* of Ego psychology (*Écrits*, p. 328) – show that he saw this analysis as shrouded in an aura of Americanism, even though Kris had not yet travelled to America. Since he was interested in passing Kris off as a fully Americanized analyst – who was betraying his noble Central European origins and those of psychoanalysis – by a kind of metonymy, Lacan also gives Prof. Brain the traits of Americanism.

All the same, in 1945, at the end of the war, Kris wanted to return to London with his family, as well as to finish his analysis with Anna Freud.[4]

As we shall see, this hasty Americanization of Kris and his patient offers us keys to a deeper – less propagandistic – understanding of the relationship between Lacan and New York ego psychology, of which Kris was the leading figure.

But what is even more interesting is that in his reconstruction of the case, Lacan leaves out an extremely important point, without which it is impossible to understand his comments fully.

Kris and his patient come to the following conclusion:

The patient had made the author [of the book he thought he had plagiarized] say what he wanted to say himself. Once this clue was secured the whole problem of plagiarism appeared in a new light. The eminent colleague [of the patient], it transpired, had repeatedly taken the patient's ideas, embellished and repeated them without acknowledgment. The patient was under the impression he was hearing for the first time a productive idea without which he could not hope to master his own subject, an idea which he felt he could not use because it was his colleague's property.

(Kris, 1951, p. 22)

This is a crucial point. The point is not so much that Prof. Brain thinks he took someone else's ideas; ideas that were in fact original, but – something far more baroque, I would say – that the relationship of plagiarism, if there was one at all, was inverted: someone else had taken Brain's ideas, and he believed that he himself was the plagiarist. Mitchell and Margaret Black (1995, p. 29) go as far as writing that the patient "was not a plagiarist but a ghostwriter".

For reasons we shall later discuss, Lacan does not emphasize this point, even though it was perfectly in line with what he'd theorized for years with regard to the "mirror stage" and what he was theorizing at that time with regard to narcissism, something that he had summed up in the formula: "language is a communication in which the sender receives his own message back from the receiver in an inverted form".[5] In our case we are not simply dealing with a message, but we do in any case find an inverted relationship: plagiarism by the other becomes one's own plagiarism, from plagiarized (passive) to plagiarist (active). This is the exact reversal of a much more common reversal, the most widespread in social relations between people: the reversal whereby the other is seen as the aggressor, while it is actually the subject who attacked first. Again and again, we see acts that are actually inverted reflections of our own acts as coming from the other. It's as if, looking at myself in a mirror, I do not recognize the image as my own reflection and see another looking back at me. . . . Here, however, in this game of mirrors, it is the subject who considers his own ideas a plagiarism, when this plagiarism instead seems to us to have been performed by the other.

Yet Lacan concludes by saying just this: "the relation to the other . . . always contains in itself this fundamental, original element of negation, which here takes the form of inversion". It is evidently a case of the active/passive inversion of plagiarism, but Lacan does not provide his audience with that important segment of Kris's analysis. Did he forget? Perhaps, but forgetfulness is a slip that a Freudian should be prompted to interpret.

Here Lacan lingers on *dénégation* – denial or disavowal – because at that session, he had invited the eminent Hegelian philosopher Jean Hyppolite to comment on Freud's brief but extremely dense essay *Die Verneinung*, which I would translate as "The Denial" rather than, as has been done, "Negation". (Note that at times Lacan uses the term *dénégation* and at other times the term *négation*. So here we should apply to Lacan the criterion that he himself often applied to Freud when he read different expressions of Freud not as synonymous but as expressing different concepts.) Lacan's word is consequently a commentary on Hyppolite's commentary. Denial is what often happens in a session, when the analysand says, for example, "I don't mean in any way to be aggressive with you", which actually means that the analysand does have the (unacknowledged) intention of being aggressive.

Thanks to denial, an unconscious truth is uttered: it gains access to the speech but only thanks to the label "not": by denying, the subject affirms; the affirmation is stated in a negative form. In this case, the denial does not take place by branding an utterance with a negative adverb but by inverting the passive relation into an active one: the plagiarized author becomes himself a plagiarist, or at least becomes convinced of being one. But precisely on the basis of what Lacan said about Brain's case, the reason for this conclusion is unclear.

Further in our discussion, we will begin to understand the reason for this missing reference. Lacan would later clearly state that plagiarism – meaning plagiarism of contents, of ideas – does not exist, because there is no such thing as private owner-ship of linguistic expressions (and this in spite of the fact that plagiarism is con-sidered illegal by the civil legislations of many countries).[6] If plagiarism does not exist, then it doesn't even make sense to say that Brain is the victim of plagiarism rather than a plagiarist. But Lacan doesn't state this clearly here: it's as if on the one hand he accepted the idea that there is an inversion from plagiarist to victim of plagiarism or vice versa, but on the other he already considers the idea irrelevant, since plagiarism does not exist.

Yet, Lacan actually did believe in plagiarism, because he repeatedly accused others of plagiarizing him. In 1953 he accused his colleague Sacha Nacht[7] of pla-giarism; then his pupil Didier Anzieu; then, in 1961, Daniel Lagache;[8] and in 1966 the philosopher Paul Ricoeur. (It must be noted that Lacan himself was accused of stealing ideas by his acknowledged teacher in psychiatry, de Clérambault).[9] How should we interpret this divide between theory and real life? As a *de facto* self-confutation?

Indeed, there are essentially two kinds of relationship between a given theory and the life of the person who theorized it: either the theory reflects the life of the theorist too much (i.e. his hopes, obsessions, desires, ideals), or the theory turns the life of the person who elaborated it upside down, as if the theory were counterbalancing life – we may think of Sartre (1964), who said "I have always thought against myself". This discrepancy has led the (Lacanian) psychoanalyst Baños Orellana (2002, p. 238) to hypothesize a kind of identification of Lacan with Prof. Brain:

> [T]here is nothing far-fetched in thinking that Lacan received from Kris's pa-tient ("I plagiarize the other") his own message in an inverted form ("the other plagiarizes me"). The man with the fresh brains is Lacan's own image in the mirror, his I (a), from which he receives the same message that applies in re-verse to a breach that has never ceased to be fresh, innovative.

Yet one notices, especially in analytic practice, what I would call a characteristic alienation of a subject's knowledge. Often, I followed patients with a psychotic subjective structure (by speaking of psychotic structure, I am, of course, already within a Lacanian perspective). Very often they would say to me "Now you're go-ing to call me crazy for saying things like that, but I'm not!" or "You believe it's my problem that I feel persecuted by X, but it's not true, the problem isn't psychological like you think: X really does persecute me". I could have said to them that I never actually said anything of the sort, that they were forming those ideas and attributing them to me. But it would have been hypocritical of me, because in fact in all those cases I'd thought exactly the things she or he attributed to me: that she was psychotic and that the persecution was her problem and not a state of reality. By refuting what I had *not* said, they were confuting the reality principle, yet they were speaking the truth. Could they read my mind? No, probably anyone would have had the same thought as me. It was they who thought all those things (true, plausible) about themselves, except they could only state and recognize them by ascribing them to the analyst. Their knowledge about themselves came from the Other, Lacan would say, but insofar as it was opposed to *their own* knowledge (the consequence of denial), the only knowledge they could assume as their own. They couldn't think, as Sartre said, against themselves: they could only conceive of the other as thinking against them.

Another example I could quote is that of an analysand, non-psychotic this time, who had undergone many years of analysis and analytic training and yet could not interpret any of her own dreams or significant acts, nor those of her patients. She seemed to lack any insight at all. For some time, I took it upon myself to tell her what I read in those dreams and acts, and she would invariably say: "I knew it! Of course, that's the way it is". But then why didn't she say so herself? Because she *knew*, but couldn't *think it* and *say it*. In this case too, saying could come to her only from the Other, and as long as the Other remained silent, she could not think/say what she already knew, not even to herself (here we perceive something of what Lacan calls "unconscious knowledge"). For her, knowledge of the unconscious (her own and that of others) was similar to our experience of our own face: we can only see it in a mirror, that is, in a place that isn't where our face actually is. We can't look at it without a specular alienation from it. This analysand could only think something if it reached her as discourse of the Other. Lacan would say that, although she had patients, she had never *authorized* herself as an analyst. It is similar with people who cannot write anything for publication, not even their PhD dissertation, because they cannot be *authors* of anything; all writings have to come from the Other.

It would seem that, according to Kris, Prof. Brain performs the reverse of a paranoid operation. I would say that he performs a melancholic operation: while the paranoiac sees in the other, although in an inverted form, what he believes and desires, on the contrary, Prof. Brain does not see what the other (the colleague) does to him, because it is he who believes that he desires and does to the other what the other desires and does.

In short, in his discussion on Kris, we find themes typical of the early Lacan: his theory of *le moi* – which here he calls the ego, as it's referred to in English – as an imaginary structure, as the integration, through the mirror image of one's self, of fragmented and uncoordinated parts; the distinction between ideal ego and ego ideal, the former being imaginary and the latter more symbolic in structure. Lacan seems to lead the case of Professor Brain back to a mirror process. Brain, by producing the discourse of plagiarism and taking it so far as to expose himself as a plagiarist in spite of himself, makes a denial. The truth of that patient consists in wanting to feed on the ideas of his ideal ego (his *grand*father), but he also exposes this truth as what he fears to do. And in what sense can we say that the symptom – the fear of stealing other people's ideas – is an inversion of his relation to the ideal ego? Where does Lacan read this inversion here?

Evidently Lacan sees it in his relationship with the books of the "eminent colleague": if it's true, as Kris writes, that his patient did not recognize *his own* ideas in those expressed by the colleague, it is because he sees his own "ideas" in the other's publications as in a mirror that is not recognized as a mirror; in short, he considers them things that belong to the other, things he does not recognize as specular. If the colleague has replaced the patient's grandfather as ideal ego, then it is no longer the colleague who mirrors the subject's ideal, but it is the subject who sees *his own* ideas as a reflection of those *of the other*. Here the game of mirrors takes on the form of a labyrinth.

It also strikes me as strange that here Lacan says – later on, as we shall see, he no longer mentions this – that he cannot understand why Kris speaks of "taking up things on the surface". In the article in which he discusses Brain, Kris intends to promote a new psychoanalytic technique, of which he sees Freud himself as the initiator. This technique aims at the analysis of resistances: instead of analysing unconscious contents directly (the *es*), the technique is to analyse first of all the resistances and defences of the patient in analysis in order to let the unconscious contents emerge gradually (defences are described as what the ego uses in life, resistances as what the patient uses in analysis). And since resistances are the work of the ego, it is necessary to begin with an analysis of the ego, that is, of its resistances. At this point the comparison with Schmideberg on the same case seems important to Kris. Schmideberg had believed Brain's words, thinking that his symptom was the compulsion to plagiarize (which, as we have seen, Kris would reverse). Schmideberg had in fact written:

> A patient who had occasionally stolen during puberty (mainly sweets and books) later showed a certain inclination to plagiarize. Since in his eyes activity was bound up with theft and scientific work with plagiarism, he could only get away from these prohibited impulses by means of a really far-reaching inhibition of his activity and intellectual work.

For her it was basically a case of kleptomania: "kids who steal will go on to steal as adults". This because, according to Kris, Schmideberg tended to interpret unconscious contents directly, in this case the impulse to steal connected to the patient's *activity* in general. Kris, on the other hand, doesn't assume his patient is really a plagiarist, so he questions him about the treatise in question: this is *the surface*. He takes an interest in what Brain thinks and what he says about the book – "superficial" elements from the analytic point of view – more than he does in his childish drives. He does deal with the latter, but after examining the surface, namely the scientific content under discussion. According to Kris, Brain's second analysis "covered a large number of details of behaviour and therefore opened the way to linking present and past, adult symptomatology and infantile fantasy". In other words, the arrow of time is reversed compared to traditional technique: He starts from the present and goes towards the past, not vice versa. The present – what the patient is doing today – is "the surface". But one may ask: was the traditional technique – Freud's in particular – really so different?

Notes

1 Heidegger (1967), part 1, chapter 5, "Ambiguity". I translate *Die Zweideutigkeit*, what the English edition translates as "ambiguity", as "misunderstanding".
2 Bruce Fink (2004), who translated Lacan into English, explains this discrepancy in the following way: "Lacan perhaps confuses 'attractive' with 'attentive' here, because he suggests in his translation that these are restaurants where one is well looked after, or well attended to (*où l'on est bien soigné*)". *Écrits*, (397.4) But is it just a question of wrong translation? From which part of Kris's text does the "spicy" or "well-seasoned food" come from?
3 I must confess to a personal disappointment. I thought I was the first to come to this conclusion. Instead, the Argentinean psychoanalyst Adela Leibovich de Duarte in 1997 reached the same conclusions.
4 See Young Bruehl (1988, p. 271).
5 *Écrits*, pp. 9, 41, 247–48, 296, 298–99, 348, 353, 438, 472, 635.
6 www.plagiarismchecker.net/is-plagiarism-illegal.php.
7 Lacan's letter to Loewenstein, 14 July 1953.
8 See Roudinesco (1986, p. 356).
9 See Roudinesco (1986, pp. 123–124).

Chapter 3

The Parrying Ego

As Kris stresses in his paper, the tantalizing novelty is the importance given to the defence mechanisms of the ego in the wake of Anna Freud's essay, *The Ego and the Mechanisms of Defence* (A. Freud, 1946). The ego-psychologists, however, were almost all native German speakers, and they were well aware that Freud's chosen term was *Abwehr*, which doesn't have the same meaning as the English *defence*. If he wanted to render that meaning, Freud would have rather used the term *Verteidigung*. *Abwehr* has more the sense of "protecting oneself from", of "avoiding a blow"; in English – as Bettelheim (2001) suggests – it would be rather *parrying* or *warding off*, or *fending off*. The original title of the quoted text by Anna Freud is *Das Ich und die Abwehrmechanismen*, which I would translate as: *The Ego and Coping Mechanisms*. The defences of the ego, which Anna Freud described one by one, are like deflectors of something that erupts from within the subject. In fact, the Ego of Freud's second topography (or of his structural model, as it is also called) can be described as a system of parries. The ego resembles a turtle that withdraws its head into its shell as soon as it feels threatened by something. In fact, in the article in question, Kris repeatedly uses the term "warding off" precisely to express the ego's parrying activity. Instead of "defence mechanism", he talks of "warding-off devices", devices for repelling.

This identification of the ego with a fencer who constantly needs to dodge blows should not come as a great surprise. If we consider our everyday activities – beyond our strictly functional ones – they seem to aim essentially at two targets: on the one hand we engineer ourselves on a daily basis to achieve forms of gratification of any kind – such as the pleasure of eating or going to mass, synagogue or mosque in order to feel good about ourselves and our conscience; on the other we are constantly engaged in averting disappointment, pain, hassles, wastes of time, embarrassments, conflicts and so on.

In fact, as in the case of Anna Freud's 1936 essay, ego psychology is also – and above all – aimed at countering the formulations of Melanie Klein and her students. The ghost of Klein, though never mentioned, looms over Kris's article, which is basically anti-Kleinian. It is as if it were saying: we "Freudians" are capable of producing innovations even more interesting than Frau Klein's! Even though Kris does not quote Klein here, he still casts her daughter Melitta's analysis in a bad

DOI: 10.4324/9781003388098-3

light, as we will see further on (in 1934, when Schmideberg published her essay, she had not yet broken with the theses of her mother).

Indeed, the Ego psychologists – who sought to be faithful followers of later developments in Freud's thought – claim that early analysis tended to interpret the contents of the *id* directly, whilst the point now is to shift focus on how the subject (the term we might use today for the Ego, on which they insist so much) engineers itself to contrast the blows of the Id, of the Super-Ego and of the outside world. In everyday terms, we all try not to be overwhelmed by our drives (particularly sexual and aggressive ones), not to be crushed by excessive obligations and feelings of guilt and to respond to the demands of our environment. Kris tries to summarize this bifurcation between the two analytic strategies by resorting to a "clinical vignette", one by Anna Freud herself, in which she speaks of a young patient of hers, a six-year-old boy:

> The visit to the dentist had been painful. During his analytic interview the little boy displayed a significant set of symptomatic actions related to this experience. He damaged or destroyed various objects belonging to the analyst, and finally repeatedly broke off the points and re-sharpened a set of pencils. How is this type of behaviour to be interpreted?
>
> The interpretation may point to retaliatory castration, may stress the turning of a passive experience into an active one, or may demonstrate that the little boy was identifying himself with the dentist and his aggression. All three interpretations can naturally be related to the anxiety which he had experienced.
>
> (Anna Freud, 1946, p. 119)

For Kris the first of the three possible interpretations could be an "id interpretation", insofar as it evokes a castration complex. His allusion to Kleinianism is clear: he talks of "retaliatory castration", and for Klein the law of retaliation, an eye for an eye, a tooth for a tooth, was very important. According to ego psychology, Kleinianism puts all its stakes on "id interpretations"; in short, it tends to revert to a primitive and – though Kris doesn't say it, he certainly suggests it – rather dogmatic form of psychoanalysis.

But the second and third interpretations, Kris says, focus on defence mechanisms – that is, on parrying. His conclusion is that "the situation allows for and ultimately requires all three interpretations". But the newest, the most interesting ones, are for him the second and third.

> The second [interpretation] emphasizes that passivity is difficult to bear and that in assuming the active role danger is being mastered. The third interpretation implements the second by pointing out that identification can serve as a mechanism of defence. . . . [This] may influence [the child] not only to react aggressively, but to achieve many goals, and may be the motivation of many aspects of his behaviour. The interpretation that stresses the mechanism of identification

is, therefore, not only the broadest, but it may also open up the largest number of new avenues, and be the one interpretation which the little boy can most easily apply in his self-observation.

(Kris, 1951, pp. 20–21)

What is Kris trying to tell us with this promotion of the ego-psychological interpretation over the id-centric?

Before answering, let's try to imagine what Lacan might have said about the child after his visit to the dentist's. Something very similar to what he says about Professor Brain, in other words exactly what Kris is here trying to promote, though with different words and concepts. What is this denial as inversion if not a different way of saying, with Anna Freud, that "the parrying machine operates by identifying the subject with the aggressor"? Just like ego psychologists, here Lacan talks about "integration of the ego", and one of the ways of integrating it is through a mirror-image reversal whereby the attacked becomes the attacker and the patient becomes the agent.

In fact, the second and third possible interpretations according to Kris seem to indicate what a Lacanian, would call imaginary inversions rather than defence mechanisms, or something similar. Lacanians, in common with many analysts of different schools, would also agree that the three possible psychoanalytic interpretations are precisely those indicated by Kris. Is the disagreement among analysts then not over content but over the metalanguage, so to speak, used to account for it? Does the main difference in this case lie mainly in the terminology, or even in the style of writing?

After any traumatic experience, all subjects, even adults, find themselves before this double path, which is ultimately only one: from being the passive object of aggression they previously were, they become the agent of aggression and therefore identify with the aggressor. The reversal from passivity to activity, and from the position of aggressed to that of aggressor, are two faces of the same inversion. In a way, by cutting off the tips of the pencils and then repairing them (I imagine with a sharpener), Anna's child was behaving more or less like Sigmund's grandson when he played *fort/da* (Freud, 1920b).[1] The latter would make a wooden reel held by a string disappear and reappear by throwing it behind one side of the cradle and then pulling it back towards him and making it re-emerge. Through this game, Sigmund's grandson was staging the disappearance and reappearance of his mother; with his activism, the child described by Anna was re-enacting an experience that had ruined his day. In both cases, a fundamental problem, which Freud did not shy away from, comes up again: what do subjects do with their traumas?

What most struck Freud was the tendency to *repeat* the trauma, even in the form of play. Why don't we just try to forget a trauma as soon as possible after we've experienced it? Why do we remain secretly attached to our traumas, why are we inclined to re-enact them, to simulate them, either in explicit aggression or in aggressive play? Or even, I would add, in perverse acts that turn the trauma into an opportunity for pure pleasure?[2] This is the basic question Freud poses, and it's in the way the various schools – Kleinian, ego-psychological, Lacanian – develop his answers, which are complex and ambiguous, that the differences between them emerge.

Notes

1 Freud, *Beyond the Pleasure Principle*. In my opinion a more adequate translation of *Jenseits des Lustprinzips* would be "Beyond the desire-pleasure principle".
2 By and large, this is the thesis I put forward in Benvenuto (2016).

Chapter 4

The Reclaiming of Death

Freud had originally said that we all repeat a trauma in order to master it. What is important for the ego is mastery (*Bemächtigung*) over what is causing it pain. This is the good, constructive side of repetition. Of course, this shift from passivity to activity also imposes a shift in the object in the case of Anna Freud's child: the victim is no longer the child but the analyst. After all, there's also a substitution of material objects: from the tooth to the pencils. In short, we elude trauma by imaginatively identifying with what traumatizes us. Ego psychology therefore pursues this aspect of Freud's analysis: if on the one hand the "parrying devices", and in particular the aggressed turning into an aggressor, are what should be analysed so that the ego is no longer forced to repeat the trauma, on the other – this is the loophole into which all ego psychology plunges – the Ego is constituted and integrated precisely through these parries. The repetition that torments the ego is also what saves it, since our daily life very often consists of constantly transmuting our *passions* (what we undergo) into *actions*. We dodge our being victims (of brutish impulses, of moral judgments, of other people's wrongdoings) by repeating, in a kind of enactment that is mostly a mere staging of our victimization. This is why these cursed dodging machines are also the blessing that allows us to live.

Now, Lacan realized at some point that his theory of the imaginary was no more than a way of saying, though with different concepts, what ego psychology was saying – with a greater international impact than Lacan, of course, whose fame at the time was rather limited. He was saying that mirror-image inversion is a constitutive defence of the subject; it is what every subject tends towards in order to integrate itself instead of being reduced into a pulp of impotence and victimhood. Therefore, in the space of less than two years, he reinterpreted Kris's case from an entirely different perspective, one supposedly irreducible to the categories of ego psychology, and his 1954 condescension towards Kris turns into open aggressiveness.[1]

Let's return to the cotton reel game, a persistent episode in psychoanalytic literature; it's continually cited because it represents a problematic crux of the theory itself. Freud doesn't only say that the playful repetition of the trauma (the transformation of the victim in agent) performs the vital and positive function of "linking" the trauma to what I would call the everyday text of psychic functioning. Further, in his discourse in *Beyond the Desire-Pleasure Principle*, Freud points out that not

DOI: 10.4324/9781003388098-4

all repetition is positive, functional, ego-syntonic or ego-reinforcing: in different ways, it is something absolutely dysfunctional, crippling, mortiferous.

On the one hand, therefore, Anna Freud's child repeats his dental trauma so as to take an active role and overcome his traumatic mortification; on the other, however – and this is the authentically new and unpalatable point of Freud's argument – this repetition is a form, Lacan was to say, *of* pure enjoyment *(jouissance)*. It is a dis-functional enjoyment given by the repetition of destruction or by the repeated de-struction, a dysfunctional pleasure, one which no cognitivist cleansing of the mind will ever be able to tame; it is a free, liberating, non-adaptive pleasure. It's as if a part of the human being – the most radical part, I would call it, the root part – fought the humiliation of falling victim to evil with the Triumph of Death. It's like the triumphant cry of joy I once heard, many years ago, in the Paris metro by a young man as he threw himself in front of the approaching train. . . . I find it hard to believe that Islamic suicide bombers who blow themselves up to kill defenceless people are merely activists who push the logic of warfare to the point of self-sacri-fice: there's a visceral attraction to death, one's own and that of others, as the Final Solution, as the only way to radically eliminate evil, which always goes hand in hand with life. *Viva la muerte*! Or, to paraphrase the futurist Marinetti (who called war the hygiene of the world), death is the hygiene of life. Now, it is this Dionysian, let's call it romantic, side of Freud's thinking that ego psychology definitely rejects. But Lacan doesn't.

But though Lacan recovers Freud's unusable thanatotic perspective, he does so while at the same time cleansing it, at least in an early phase. Lacan would say on many occasions that repetition expresses the establishment of the symbolic order, which is therefore in itself mortiferous. It is through repetition that human be-ings jump from a mere event to a symbol: by repeating an event, they transform it into a signifier. Consider the earliest words of an infant, which consist mostly of the simple repetition of a sound, a morpheme. "Boom" is the sound of a rifle, so "boom-boom" becomes the word for rifle. "Meow" is the sound cats make, so "meow-meow" becomes the name for cat. And "ma-ma", "pa-pa", "poo-poo", "wee-wee", and almost every other childish word, is repetition of the same sound. Children learn to talk by repeating a morpheme. Of Anna Freud's child, Lacan could have said that it was significant that he broke the tips of pencils, that is, tools used for writing. The point is that he blunted them and then sharpened them again: *Fort/da*. The pencils are tools for writing, but by breaking them and making them sharp again, he wrote something himself. . . . What did he write? He wrote himself, his human destiny, the fact that our life will always be a passive being broken, which we will transform by "breaking Iraq's back" or "breaking Ukraine's back", only to then regret it and recompose it. By so doing we symbolize our existence, we give it a temporary sense, we inscribe it in a cycle of destruction and reconstruc-tion, of annihilation and reappearance. In short, Lacan seems to be saying, Freud's death drive also has a silver lining: being the matrix of the symbolic, it is also the lifeblood of our humanity.

But isn't this yet another domestication of Freud's ultimate, radical thought? Of the admission that there is something mortiferous beyond sense and beyond life, the silent workings of disintegration, of entropy? In fact, Lacan had said that primordial symbolization was *Bejahung*, affirmation, of when we ingest the good thing and turn it into our own representation or re-presentation. But on the other hand, in a contradictory way – for a Hegelian like Lacan, indulging in contradictions is just fine – the symbolic is originated precisely by the senseless repetition, the vacuous insistence of acts themselves. In this way, Lacan, too – though in a different way from ego psychology – ends up defusing the Freudian Thanatos: death ceases to be the final silence that surrounds us and becomes a throb, an interval, a moment that will prove constructive. In Lacan there is certainly an *Aufhebung* of death, that is to say, at once a lifting up, erasure and conservation, its transubstantiation into life, into signifying breath.

Note

1 Jean Allouch links the references to Kris's case to the institutional crisis in which Lacan was one of the protagonists. The 1954 reference to Prof. Brain occurs shortly after the IPA had created an advisory committee to study negotiations with the Société Française de Psychanalyse (SFP), of which Lacan was a member, in order to decide whether to admit it to the IPA. See Jean Allouch, "Jacques Lacan's analysant" in Baños Orellana (2002, p. 245).

Chapter 5

Acting Out and *Passage à l'acte*

On 11 January 1956, Lacan returned to this case in his seminar on *The Psychoses* (*Sem 3*, 79–81). Now he attacked above all the concept of "defence" in relation to delusions: the idea that delusions are basically one of the subject's defences. What does Professor Brain have to do with a psychotic delusion? We are about to find out.

> This concept [of defence] is so insistent, so tempting, precisely because it touches something objectifiable. The subject defends, well then! We will help him to understand that he does nothing but defend, we will show him what he is defending against. . . . [I]f you have the feeling that the subject is defending against something that you yourself see and that he doesn't, if, that is, you clearly see that the subject is aberrant with respect to reality, then the notion of defence is insufficient to enable you to place the subject before reality.
>
> (*Sem 3*, 79)

Lacan recounted again Brain's closing remark on fresh brains on the menu. But while he thinks Kris considers that kind of response a confirmation of the correctness of his interpretation, Lacan has a different opinion:

> Kris has pressed the right button. It is not enough to press the right button. The subject quite simply *acts out*.
>
> (*Sem 3*, 80)

In psychoanalytic jargon, *acting out* is an act or series of acts, even aggressive in character, towards others or oneself, the presumably symbolic value of which the acting subject is not aware of. It is *an act that wants to state something*. The term refers specifically to acts of people in analysis. Certain things, rather than being *said* to the analyst, are *acted* outside the consulting room. "We think it most undesirable – Freud wrote – if the patient *acts* outside the transference instead of remembering".[1] For Lacan, what Freud calls *remembering* is the ability of the analysand to *talk* to the analyst about something that matters.

DOI: 10.4324/9781003388098-5

An acting out can occur in an analytical session, and in that case it is referred to as an *acting in*.

In Brain's case, the acting out seems to consist in the fact he went out to eat fresh brains after Kris offered him his interpretation. But an analysis of Kris's text has already shown us there is no acting out here.

In fact, as in the 1954 seminar, Lacan falls into the same misconception: he thinks Brain went in search of fresh brains after the previous session, while instead – as we saw – this was a habit of his after every session. Is an act that is regularly repeated still an acting out? The thesis Lacan then developed – that the patient told Kris by way of an action "you really missed the point!" – is based on this misunderstanding of Kris's text.

We also notice something that Lacan does not: Mr. Brain doesn't actually say he eats fresh brains, he merely says that he looks at the menus, "in one of the restaurants in X street I usually find my preferred dish – fresh brains" (Kris, 1951, p. 23). We could imagine that what gives Brain pleasure is not eating that particular dish but finding it written in a restaurant menu. Would merely looking for a menu be an acting out, too? It's as if he devoured not the brains but, with his eyes, their name. Here, too, it could have something to do with his relationship to writing, as it does in the case of his presumed plagiarism.

The difference in tone towards Kris between the Lacan of 1954 and the Lacan of 1956 reveals an ambivalence towards him and his method. He seems to envy a certain clinical freedom on the part of the "Americanized" analyst, who disregards the rules of the classical setting and *passe à l'acte*, takes action (engages him in what today many call the analyst's *enactment*): according to Lacan, Kris is presented with the book by his patient, reads it and comments on it. But, as we saw, this enactment is actually an invention of Lacan's. It's quite paradoxical that Lacan, who would later be de facto expelled from the IPA for his clinical misdemeanours, reproaches Kris here for a clinical breach, for an act. In fact, we also noticed another distortion: Lacan makes Kris say that the confession of acting out (the fresh brains meal) is an effect of Kris's own acting out; basically the analyst, by acting – by serving as reader-arbitrator between texts – obtained access to the word through action. It is by acting that, paradoxically, the analyst brings the other's acting into analytical speech (again according to Lacan's interpretation). But the point is that all this was largely constructed by Lacan: as in a projective test, he reads his own analytical ideal in Kris's text.

Let us return to Lacan's 1956 seminar:

> I treat acting out as equivalent to a hallucinatory phenomenon of the delusional type that occurs when you symbolize prematurely, when you address something in the order of reality and not within the symbolic register.
>
> (*Sem 3*, p. 80)

We will see what psychotic delusions and acting out have in common, but Lacan doesn't mean here that Mr. Brain is psychotic but that acting out in analysis has a structural affinity with delusion.

If Mr. Brain is a neurotic, it is therefore very likely that his plagiarism is phantasmatic. There is no need, in short – Lacan seems to be saying – for the analyst to read and analyse the book in question (at the level of reality) to understand that this patient is an imaginary plagiarist. And indeed, when Kris does so, the patient "testifies that something emerges from reality that is obstinate, something that imposes itself upon him" and hence that saying to him "you are not a plagiarist!" is a naive psychotherapeutic move, to which the subject reacts with an acting out. The patient, in other words, "shows you what is at stake by making you eat fresh brains". Here Lacan certainly makes a very bold move: with his punch line about the brains, the subject would have the analyst symbolically eat those very brains. What goes around comes around: Kris acted by reading the book, Brain acts by eating (or reading in turn?) the brains. There is a point of fluctuation and perplexity.

Lacan is ultimately reproaching Kris for having made the amateurish mistake of trying to correct the patient's view of reality. This is something with which those who supervise trainee psychotherapists are very familiar. One example of many: a girl continually accuses her mother of having ruined her life by having her undergo an operation that she believes was unsuccessful and aggravated her condition. Her psychologist knows by other means that it was not her mother who insisted on surgery but the doctors. And she tells her so: "It's not your mother who wanted you to have that operation". The result is only to exasperate the patient, who perceives the psychologist as an ally of her hated mother. This trivial error is the result of a prejudice from which psychologists find it hard to free themselves: that the ethical function of the shrink is to correct the patient's distorted image of reality as much as possible.

But it is also true that if in the course of the analysis the girl in question gradually begins to diverge from her initial idea; that is, she realizes that the other who is persecuting her is one thing and the Other as mother is something else, this can be hailed as progress in the analysis. What ceases is what I would call the paranoidization of the Other, the tendency to see a persecutory other in what Lacan calls the Other, that is, the symbolic instance that the subject interprets in a persecutory key. I would say that a large part of an analysis resolves itself precisely in this: in subjects ceasing to spend their lives condemning others, in particular their parents. They are finally distracted from the ever-resumed hunt for the cause/blame of their discontent. In a way, the end of analysis coincides with a reconciliation with the real parents.

In short, for Lacan it seems to be completely irrelevant whether Prof Brain seeks to be cured because he *imagines* he is forced to plagiarize or because he *is forced* to plagiarize. Initially this difference is indeed irrelevant, but as the analysis proceeds, the shift in the subject's position is hailed: he is no longer confronted with the compulsion to plagiarize but with the compulsion to believe he is plagiarizing. Unless he is a psychotic, that is, unless the belief he is plagiarizing in the real (but is plagiarism something that happens in the real?) is in fact a delusion. In fact, a delusion always consists in seeing how *to carry out* in the real a mere *thinking that*.

And, indeed, the fact that Lacan puts his finger on Brain's oral foreclosure is an indication that Lacan considers him basically a psychotic.

Hence the entirely different way in which we can consider Brain's account of his eating (or imagining eating?) fresh brains. Kris ends his clinical report with that account arguably to show how the deconstruction of superficial beliefs serves precisely to arrive at what Lacan considers essential, the unconscious oral drive aimed at devouring another's mind. Once Prof Brain has accepted the viewpoint that he does not *carry out* but *thinks that* (that he does not plagiarize but thinks he has plagiarized), he cannot escape any confrontation with his unconscious representations.

But, above all, Lacan's interpretation of Brain's act is based on a flawed reading of Kris, as we saw. His interpretative fabrication has no basis in fact.

Still, Lacan concludes with some ambiguous remarks:

Is there something that he shows? I would go further – I would say that there is nothing at all that he shows, but that something shows itself.

It is not the ego of the subject that shows itself, instead through the symptom and the acting out, some *thing* shows itself. But this thing is no-thing. What then is this no-thing? Lacan would provide an answer to this question a few months later in one of his essays.

But before going to this other 1956 text, we will jump ahead to 1963, to the seminar *Anxiety* (*Se10*, pp. 146–7). Here Lacan returns again to Prof. Brain to illustrate the difference between *acting out* and *passage à l'acte*. He introduces this second concept with regard to the case of the homosexual girl described by Freud (1920a). This girl, caught by her father in the street in the company of the lady with whom it is public knowledge that she is in love, runs towards the parapet of the bridge under which a railway passes and throws herself off it, albeit saving herself. This letting oneself fall, this leaving the scene (of the world), is for Lacan a *passage to the act*. It makes present what Lacan calls object *a*, that is, an object dropped away from the scene, a non-representable object that in this case *falls outside* the social framework. A similar passage to the act, according to Lacan, is the slap that Dora delivers to her admirer, Mr K., on the lakeside after he tells her "*ich habe nichts an meiner Frau*", "I get nothing out of my wife".[2] Dora will leave Mr. K's company after this slap. Both ladies pass on to the act in the sense that they disappear from the sight of the Other.

Again, with reference to the two female cases, Lacan recognizes an acting out. In the case of the young homosexual, "the whole adventure with the woman of doubtful reputation, who is raised to the function of supreme object, is an acting-out". As for Dora, her entire paradoxical behaviour in the K. household is an acting out. That is to say, acting out is essentially putting on a show, a *montrage*. If the passage to the act out is a leaving the scene, acting out is what I would call a staging. Here Lacan seems to be referring to the other sense of the verb *to act*, in the sense of an actor performing. And it is at this point in his elaboration of the distinction that Lacan evokes Prof. Brain:

> Kris . . . wants to reduce [his patient] by means of the truth; he shows him in the most irrefutable fashion that he is not a plagiarist; he has read his book; his book is well and truly original, on the contrary it is the others who have copied him. The subject cannot contest it. Only he does not give a damn about it. And on leaving, what is he going to do? As you know . . . he goes and eats fresh brains.
>
> (*Se10*, p. 147)

It is incredible how in the space of a few lines he piles up a set of distortions, even though he has partly corrected them in the past! Later I shall make clear that in fact Kris and Brain are not talking about the latter's book but about the book Brain thinks he copied. That therefore Kris has not read anything directly. That it is not "the others" who copy him, but probably just one person, his favourite colleague. And of course, he does not go and eat fresh brains after that session; it is merely something he has done repeatedly in the past.

Now, Lacan adds: "With the fresh brains, the patient simply waves to Ernst Kris. Everything you tell me is true, only it leaves the question unscathed; there are still fresh brains. In order to show you, I am going to eat some when I leave in order to tell you about it the next time". According to Lacan, fresh brains are Brain's object *a*, "the pound of flesh", as Lacan calls it (with a reference to *The Merchant of Venice*), something dense that cannot be symbolized or imagined. But eating fresh brains in order to tell the analyst is precisely a staging, a putting-on-a-scene, as is said in French (*mise-en-scène*), in order to tell the analyst something. "Acting out is a symptom", Lacan says. But as soon as he says it, he distinguishes between acting out and symptom: the former needs to be interpreted, the latter not necessarily. This is because according to Lacan, the symptom is *jouissance*; it does not need the Other – one suffers from symptoms independently of analysis, whereas acting out is like a message to a recipient, namely the analyst. Indeed, Lacan specifies that "acting out is the primer of transference". It is wild transference. And managing transference then consists precisely of taming this wild transference that acting out represents, "just as you would put a horse in a jousting exhibition" – an observation that today wouldn't fail to spark an ethical, so to speak, debate.

All this is very interesting; the difference between acting out and passage to the act is eloquent, suggestive, engaging. Unfortunately, in this case it is based on a complete distortion by Lacan of the text he draws on.

Now, since we do not derive our own enjoyment from bringing Lacan down from the pedestal on which so many have placed him, it is not enough for us to merely point out the distortion once more. We also want to ask ourselves *what* – we almost feel like saying: *which* object *a* – prompts Lacan to illustrate an important thesis of his from a distortion of someone else's text. Since it is not a case of a one-off lapsus but of a systematic misunderstanding of the text, we ask ourselves: what was it that gave him so much enjoyment, I won't say in Kris's text, but in the image he had created for himself of this case and of its relationship with the analyst? We shall try to provide an answer further on.

Notes

1 Sigmund Freud (1940 [1938]).
2 Freud, 1905b (*SE* 7, p. 98. *GW* 5, S. 261). Lacan's translation into French of these words is "my wife is nothing to me". A discussion on Lacan's way of understanding Mr. K.'s sentence would take us very far, as surely there is also some distortion here somewhere.

Chapter 6

Foreclosed Orality

When in March 1956 Lacan revised his seminar for the journal *La psychanalyse*, he also extended his commentary on Brain's case; it takes up no less than seven dense pages.

Some ask: which was delivered/written first, the seminar of 11 January 1956, or the text published in March 1956? The most probable hypothesis is that these are two almost simultaneous elaborations. This is not a question of mere pedantry, because in the two cases Lacan reports Kris's text in two entirely different ways. In the spoken seminar, Lacan distorts Kris's account in the way we have seen, while strangely enough, this does not happen in the publication that came out two months later! In the printed version he faithfully reports Kris's text, but – amazingly – accepts and expands on the conclusions that were based on the distorted version. That is, he distorts when speaking to an audience, while he rectifies when publishing in a journal. So why does he radicalize his interpretation of the eating fresh brains as an acting out in the published text, when we have just seen that this interpretation is based on an erroneous reconstruction? The labyrinth becomes more intricate.

It should also be noted that in the published version, even though it is more faithful to Kris's text, Lacan changes his tone completely: he now openly derides Kris's approach.

This acting out, Lacan says, undoubtedly has a transferential significance – meaning by this that the brains he gobbles up greedily are symbolically those of the analyst? And he adds:

> But what can we make of the act itself if not a true emergence of a primordially *"retranchée"* ["excised"] oral relation, which no doubt explains the relative failure of his first analysis?
>
> (*Écrits*, p. 332)

This remark is Lacan's essential contribution – in 1956 – to Kris's case, a contribution we shall comment on later, since it brings into play a concept that was to become increasingly important in Lacanian thought, what he at that time called *retranchement* and would later call *forclusion*, foreclosure. Both terms translate Freud's *Verwerfung*.

DOI: 10.4324/9781003388098-6

The English translation *foreclosure* is accurate, as both *forclusion* and *foreclosure* are terms from administrative law that refer to losing the right to use something that belongs to me: if my house is in foreclosure, I no longer have the right to set foot inside it. As we shall see, *foreclosure* refers to the impossibility, for a subject, of using a signifier, which is "supposed to be" theirs. In this case, according to Lacan, a signifier connected to orality has been foreclosed.

Lacan doesn't tell us, however, what the foreclosure of orality implies in the case in question. Now, Lacan said that what is suppressed or foreclosed in the symbolic returns in the real. By *real* he doesn't mean what in both common and philosophical discourse refers to reality as external to subjectivity, such as the world surrounding us. The real at play here is *what emerges as real for a subject*. This return into the real takes, for example, the form of hallucination: in this case the subject confidently situates within the real something that for us (who are not hallucinating) appears instead as imaginary. Similarly, the real appears in sensations known – by antithesis – as *derealization*, when habitual, domestic reality seems to lose its consistency and subjects find themselves in an alien, enigmatic reality. The real therefore appears whenever we have the sensation of an interruption in the realistic course of things. In spite of this, by *real* Lacan also means what we commonly (or philosophically) call reality, specifically when a symbol appears in external, habitual reality. This is what happens in acting out: the fact that a symbolic question is acted out in reality situates this reality in the position of the real. This is indeed the case with Professor Brain.

It is as if Lacan were saying: Brain failed to symbolize a relationship of oral devouring; therefore this devouring relationship returns for him in reality, in the sense that he *really* thinks he is stealing/eating other people's ideas. Stealing ideas from others is not a metaphor here (as the case would be in a neurotic return of the repressed) but a conviction, however delusional: it is as if ideas became so real that you could take them or leave them, eat them or spit them out. Without going as far as saying that Brain is psychotic, Lacan sees in him a process that is indeed typical of psychosis: what is foreclosed in the symbolic returns as experiences in the real.

But let us look now at some further discrepancies between the source text and Lacan's reading of it.

Lacan repeats the description of the case, and when he says that according to Brain the colleague's book already says everything he wanted to say, he writes:

[Kris] asks to see the book from the library. He reads it. He discovers that nothing in it justifies what the subject thinks is in it. It is the subject alone who has attributed to the author everything the subject himself wanted to say.

Now, this is a totally corrupted interpretation of what Kris actually wrote, which is:

His paradoxical tone of satisfaction and excitement led me to inquire in very great detail about the text he was afraid to plagiarize.

And so "in a process of extended scrutiny, it turned out that . . ."

Basically, this inquiry into the text seems to have taken place verbally during the session. The analysand himself supplies the analyst with a version of the text that doesn't point to any form of plagiarism. One wonders why Lacan imagines Kris actually *reading* the book. We notice that Lacan refers to the text in question as an *article*, while Kris actually calls it a *treatise* (*Sem* 1, p. 59).

It must be noted that it is precisely this biased reading of Lacan that authorized him to write that the "intellectual profession" of Prof. Brain "appears to be, in the glimpses one catches of it, not far removed from what might be our preoccupations" (*Sem 1*, p. 59). Indeed, if Kris did read Brain's colleague's article, and if he realized early enough that it was not a case of plagiarism, this means it was a field Kris was familiar with, namely (apart from art history) psychoanalysis. Lacan insinuates, without saying so, that Prof. Brain was an analyst in training, in short, a future colleague of Kris. But this abductive reasoning makes no sense if in fact Kris did not read the article (which was, rather, a treatise).

As the Italians say, "*traduttore traditore*", "the translator is a traitor", but in this case we should also add that the "reader is an evildoer": betrayal or wrongdoing are inevitable insofar as anyone who reads also interprets. To interpret is to "eat" what we read or listen to, that is, to make *our own* something that was previously *other*. So, we can say of someone that he found a book or a system of ideas *hard to digest*. Hence Lacan's attempt to "eat" Kris (In Italian to *eat an opponent* also means "to defeat them easily", "to thrash them", which is also the sense of what Lacan wanted to achieve with Kris). An authentic devouring of Kris by Lacan is what stands out in this text. Memory confers even to things that have just been read or seen a "good form", that is, the sense one wants to find in these things. And what was "good form" here for Lacan was what allowed him to mock Kris as naïve, making him come across as a someone who thinks that by reading an article (which was actually a hefty volume!), you can really discern the distinction between what was "taken" from an author and what was "given" to him. And this is especially striking in a case as tricky as this one, in which we really don't know who plagiarized whom.

Among the commentators who noticed the major discrepancies between Kris's text and Lacan's commentary (for example, Darian Leader, 1997), we find Bruce Fink (2004), who reconstructs the case from a Lacanian school perspective. He admits that, on the basis of what Kris writes, we do not have a situation in which the analyst is reading the book and comparing it to the patient's own impressions. But he writes:

> Whether Lacan is right and Kris went to the library or whether Kris simply asked the patient about the texts is ultimately only a question of degree, then, for in both cases Kris's concern is with how things stand in reality: did he or did he not really plagiarize, and thus is there or is there not an ego defence against seeing that he in fact does not plagiarize?
>
> (Fink, 2004, p. 55)

I don't believe, however, that it is only a question of degree; it is also one of substance. There's a very big difference between Kris telling the patient authoritatively but above all domineeringly, "Look, you never plagiarized anything! I can assure you", and analyst and analysand, thanks to a joint subtle verbal reconstruction, reaching the conclusion – together – that perhaps there had been no plagiarism. And we could prove that the latter approach is the one Freud adopted again and again with his patients, no more nor less than Kris.

It suffices to mention the Rat Man and the way this obsessional patient would speak about his debt to a person to whom he owed a down payment for a pair of pince-nez sent to him by post (Freud, 1909b). The initial description by the patient doesn't seem to hold up, so Freud makes him tell the story no less than three times – how do you describe that if not as an *extended scrutiny*? Freud dedicates many pages to the reconstruction of this strange episode of debt on the part of the Rat Man, and it is only at the end that Freud realizes how the patient had (unknowingly) distorted the events he had told him, and that the person he had to repay was, in fact, the clerk at the post office where the pince-nez had arrived.

It is only by taking up things "from the surface" – a minor hitch with the person to whom the Rat Man had to repay a small sum he'd spent as a down payment – that Freud reaches the core of the subject's problem: that of an unpayable debt, so to speak, one that the obsessional subject has to pay back *to the letter*. Freud comes to this with his patient just as Kris does with Brain. If Kris can be accused of anything, it's that he presents as a great technical innovation what Freud had always practised from the very beginning.

The fact is that in 1958 Lacan himself would say something very similar when he spoke of "the rectification of the subject's relation with the real" (*Écrits*, p. 500). Now, this sentence was to become highly successful among Lacanians, many of whom remark that "analysis leads to a rectification of the subject's relation with the real". In fact, Lacan used this phrase once, in the *Écrits*, in reference to an early initial phase of an analysis. It's worth quoting in full the paragraph in which the fatidic phrase appears:

> What I am saying is that it is in a direction of the treatment, ordered, as I have just shown, according to a process that goes from the rectification of the subject's relation with the real to the development of the transference and then to interpretation, that there is situated the horizon within which Freud made the fundamental discoveries, which we are still living off, about the dynamics and the structure of obsessional neurosis. Nothing more, but nothing less either.
>
> (*Écrits*, p. 500)

Here Lacan also refers to the Rat Man: Freud works first with a rectification of the subject's relations to the real in order to establish a transference and then – only after a transference has been established – moves on to interpretations. But how does this "rectification" of the subject's relation with the real differ from Kris's "taking things up from the surface"?

It would be easy to show that Freud (1905b) behaves in a very similar way with Dora, for example. Here too a turning point occurs when Dora has to admit that she herself was an accomplice – in real life – in the love affair between her father and Mrs. K., a relationship that she later denounced as unbearable for her.

Thinking that the analyst shouldn't question reality – as Lacan seems to be saying here – would be a sign of psychoanalytic fundamentalism. The position of every analyst – and of Lacan, too, I am convinced of it – is that of reliable witness to reality; this is part of the game. This is the attitude especially taken in relation to any sort of delusion. What makes us think that a patient is delusional if not the established fact that a delusion is such because it doesn't correspond to reality? Lacan, who worked for many years as a psychiatrist, must have known this well enough. Obviously, it is not a question of telling the patient "You are being delusional" but of listening to what they're saying using the delusional hypothesis as a key. And some cases may be in doubt: is this subject being delusional or not? Not in the general sense that perhaps every delusion bespeaks some reality but in the common, down-to-earth sense that sometimes we cannot tell the extent to which a discourse really is delusional.

Let us take the cases of hysterical hypochondria that we come across at every turn. In these cases subjects cling tooth and nail to the shreds of some apparently organic disorder, taking multiple medical tests because none of them come up with "the answer" that they are looking for (but what answer are they looking for, in fact?) and dogmatically and fiercely reject any allusion to the mental character of their disorder. So, for months, a woman, an expert in psychoanalysis, suffering from the most classical hysterical lump – something is blocking her throat and food won't go down – embarks on a long sequence of tests, convinced that her complaint is a matter for laryngologists, not for psychoanalysts. In the same way as it's dangerous to contradict a delirious psychotic, we should never say to a hypochondriac "go see a shrink"! It's clear that in these cases too the analyst acts on the basis of a supposed knowledge: that the physical disorder is a signifying expression, that the treatment to be carried out will focus on the symbolic, not on the organic, reality. Even if analysts are not obliged to disclose this knowledge to their patient – which their subjects would in any case reject – it is on the basis of this knowledge (which analysts suppose they possess) that they plan their interventions. In other words, the idea that analysts should set aside any knowledge and simply follow the speech of the analysand without any prejudices is a pipe dream: the analyst adopts a certain position starting from a form of non-psychoanalytic knowledge, "common sense" in a broad sense, which entails that position. And this is precisely what many critics of psychoanalysis "on the left", from Foucault to Deleuze, have blamed it for: the fact that the analyst, like the psychiatrist, continues to operate from a position of power and knowledge.

One might say that what Lacan reproaches Kris with is not the fact of having discovered that Professor Brain in fact does not plagiarize but of having convinced him of this as a matter of fact. In a certain sense, Lacan seems to say that Kris should have kept this belief to himself. This is why Lacan reads the account of the meal of fresh brain as a way of communicating with the analyst, "I'm not interested in what you say!" For Lacan, it is not relevant; it makes no difference whether the patient knows that he is not in fact plagiarizing or whether he continues to think that he is being forced to plagiarize. It's as if his unconscious were saying to Kris, "Even if I believe I plagiarize without actually doing it, the fact remains that I need to eat other people's brains! I truly enjoy it!" That is, plagiarizing is his enjoyment, even though it is imaginary. Similarly, for Lacan, it is useless to say to a hypochondriac "Look you're not really sick!" He might continue to think that he needs an MD, not a psychoanalyst. (But then, how could the psychoanalyst ever persuade the patient to analyse himself, rather than having another doctor prescribe more tests?)

Who is right, Kris or Lacan? Is it necessary first to confront a subject with reality, or is it better to put it in brackets and deal with unconscious complexes without addressing the denial of reality?

These are indeed two different strategies, but is it possible to say, a priori, that one strategy is good while the other is bad? It's somewhat similar to the art of war: is there a unique optimal strategy for each type of battle? If this were the case, our strategy would soon be known to the opponent, and it would be easy for him to counter it. In actual fact, a unique strategy must be conceived for each battle. Similarly, in analysis, everything depends on whom you are dealing with. In this sense, Kris and Lacan, insofar as they suggest that their strategy is valid *always, everywhere* and *with everyone*, are both wrong.

The difference is that Kris has a decisive advantage over Lacan in promoting his strategy: Prof. Brain was his own analysand, and he therefore knew him much better than Lacan could ever know him, especially since the latter was relying on an account that he had largely misunderstood. In any case, both analysts seem on the verge of dogmatism.

Chapter 7

The Property of Ideas

After Kris has verbalized his discovery to the patient, he says to him: "Only the ideas of others were truly interesting, only ideas one could take". And Lacan continues with his translation of Kris's article, which I have here translated back into English:

> At this point of the interpretation I was waiting for the patient's reaction. The patient was silent and the very length of the silence, *insofar as it was commensurate **with** the effects of my interpretation*, had a special significance. Then, as if reporting a sudden insight, he said: "Every noon, when I leave here, before luncheon, and before returning to my office, I walk through X Street (a street, as the author tells us, well known for its small attractive restaurants, and where you are treated in a special way) and I look at the menus in the windows. In one of the restaurants I usually find my preferred dish – fresh brains.

This time Lacan's quote is accurate: "Every noon", with no implication that he went to eat fresh brains only after Kris's interpretation. But, as we have already seen, this correction doesn't prevent him from continuing to act out his thesis.

I highlighted some words in bold and italics because they're not present in the original text: Lacan interpolated them. They're his invention. But why did he do so? Did it make the context easier to read? I don't believe so. Kris limited himself to saying that the length of the patient's silence had "a special significance" but without saying what it meant, while Lacan makes him say that it was *evidently* an effect of his interpretation. Whereas Kris suspends the sense of what he is saying, Lacan precipitates him into an enunciation.

In short, Lacan is suggesting that this confession appears to Kris as a clear confirmation of his own approach – adding that the mountain (and the method Kris is trying to promote) has given birth to a mouse. In other words, Lacan's interpolation serves to ascribe to Kris a claim which, in fact, his rival does not express in his text: that Professor Brain's confession was an effect of Kris's interpretation and thus a validation of his method based on the "analysis of defences". Instead, as we've seen, for Lacan the confession/acting out makes something more fundamental emerge: Brain's suppression or foreclosure of orality.

DOI: 10.4324/9781003388098-7

This biased reading of the original also allows Lacan to focus on what he aims to reject of the New York school, on the ethical level in particular: the fact that the analyst assumes the role of determining what is true and what is not – and therefore also the thoughts that were taken and those that were given. For Lacan the analysis of defences boils down to this: convincing the patient that the analyst is right, that the analyst knows the truth and that the only way to recognize the unconscious is to accept the analyst's point of view. If the patient doesn't accept an interpretation by the analyst, the latter will retort: "You are resisting!", as in religious proselytism, where if someone does not adhere to the new faith, they are "resisting the truth", probably through the work of the devil, except that it was difficult for Lacan to demonstrate this prevarication of the analyst on the basis of this particular case, hence the distortion. In fact, in this way, he attributes to Kris's expression "extended scrutiny" the most caricatural sense: Kris makes the patient provide him with a copy of the book, he reads it (admitting it relates to a scientific field in which he is competent) and then says to the patient, "It's not true that this colleague of yours has appropriated and exploited your ideas!" If that had been the case, it would be laughable. Besides, in order to make a comparison, Kris would have needed to be acquainted with the patient's ideas, something which can't be taken for granted. Instead, everything suggests that the scrutiny was actually carried out above all by the analysand and that all that was left for the analyst to do was to draw the consequences. Moreover, Lacan relates this conclusion in direct speech, whereas Kris gives it in indirect speech; that is, Kris does not distinguish between what he, the analyst, said and what the patient said: they come to the conclusion that the plagiarism was imaginary together.

In other words, it seems clear that Kris never read the treatise, but suspected – unlike Schmideberg – that the conviction of having plagiarized the other was an illusion. And that therefore, by questioning the patient, he led him to recognizing that things were different from what he had thought. What else can we call this if not a rectification of the real?

Now, this is an issue that any analyst raises whenever a patient, even a psychotic one, describes the behaviour of others. To what extent should the description be taken literally? If an analysand says that his mother is a hag who despises him, to what extent is it a subjective interpretation? This is one reason family therapy has been so successful in certain countries: here you don't depend on what parents say about their children or what children say about the parents, or spouses about each other, but you can watch them interact in the flesh. Alas, patients often talk about relationships from the past with parents who are dead or extremely elderly, and a psychotherapist cannot conjure up ghosts through a medium. Should analysts then be unconcerned with how realistic a given representation of others about whom they know nothing may be?

If Lacan had respected the text strictly, he wouldn't have had an opportunity to pose the question that was crucial to him: *what is the sense of plagiarism?* The concept of plagiarism implies that of intellectual property, something Lacan does not believe in. Therefore, "plagiarism doesn't exist. There is no symbolic property"

(*Sem 3*, p. 80). This is an essential point of philosophy (particularly of Heideggerian philosophy, from which he took his cue): no one has the ownership of a language. We learn language from others since childhood, and therefore, to some extent, we plagiarize what others say to us. A language is the discourse of the Other. Even our own ideas always come to us from others. We can of course (rarely) develop something original, but always starting from a ripping-off of what has already been said and written. Not unlike what I'm doing in this very text, that is, plagiarizing – if plagiarism existed – Kris and Lacan.

(We do not have the space here to discuss the debate in legal thinking surrounding plagiarism, though it is of great interest.[1] It is understood as a definition of copyright. Copyright was recognized by many countries at the 1886 Berne International Convention, but in fact each country has its own specific laws. There has been much debate about whether to equate plagiarism with theft – a theft of signifiers rather than objects – and on *what* in a text or piece of music can be the object of plagiarism. A distinction is therefore made between the content of a work, pointing out that the content does not belong to the author since, once a work is published, it belongs to everyone, and the precise form it assumes. In short, plagiarism becomes an offence insofar as it is limited to the signifiers, and in this sense the plagiarism for which Prof. Brain blames himself is completely outside the legal domain. Also worthy of note is the fact that the French word *plagiat* is used to mean "being inspired by an aesthetic model in general or imitating a style", a sense that perhaps influenced Lacan's interpretation.)

A personal anecdote. I have a country house near a village where the League – the party that is xenophobic and fascist leaning – obtained over 50% of the vote years ago. One of my neighbours is an elderly affable farming woman who, though uncultivated, is by no means stupid. A woman incapable of any kind of evil. She is also very pious – but she distrusts Pope Francis because she thinks that he supports immigrants. In that village there are several foreigners, all affluent or wealthy, who bought a second home there; in fact, there are no poor immigrants. Our neighbour has very good relations with these "respectable" foreigners. . . . Yet she too voted for the League and says that immigration is a scourge. When I pointed out to a local friend, a cultured person, that even a good-natured woman like my neighbour can be a racist, she replied: "But it's not what she really thinks, she's simply repeating what she hears in the village, what the others thin". And I replied: "*Everyone*, including ourselves, ultimately does nothing but repeat what others say . . . except that our 'others' are not xenophobic". She laughed, admitting that this was perfectly true.

We all repeat what we hear in the village, even if it's a village of psychoanalysts and philosophers. And only occasionally do some of us manage to say something out of line, something that, for that very reason, it is very difficult to get through to others. As long as we repeat the thoughts and words of our tribe, the other members accept us and we don't run into any problems.

In other eras people wrote because they were inspired: either by the Muses for the pagans, or by God or the Holy Spirit for the Christians.

Sing, O goddess, the anger of Achilles son of Peleus . . .

(beginning of the *Iliad*)

Still today we say "I am inspired" or "I can't find any inspiration". Today we're accustomed since childhood to thinking according to the metaphysical concept that ideas come from within us, but for centuries it was seen as obvious that it was the other way around: ideas came from the Other, be it a Muse, God, or an angel.

Today many writers say that they somehow feel that things and characters come to them and use them to find their spoken word. The world *dictates* the right words to the author. This happens in painting, too.

Lacan became particularly interested in Brain's case because he must have found it very "Lacanian". The drama of an intellectual who won't publish anything because he feels he needs to steal the ideas of others raised the question of intellectual property, that is, the relationship between subject and symbolic. We can all speak and write in an original way, true. Noam Chomsky reminded us that even a four-year-old can articulate sentences in his own language that no one has ever articulated before. And Wilhelm von Humboldt had already described language as "The infinite use of finite means".[2] A language is a matrix of new utterances *ad infinitum*. Yet, for Lacan language is never "one's own" but Other's. There is no private language (as Wittgenstein also stated)[3] nor any private property of a language. We always speak the language of others, even when we only speak to ourselves. And also our ideas, insofar as they are creatures of language, are not ours. More generally, we steal our ideas from language. Talking and writing basically consist of copying each other. A famous Italian comedy actor, Totò, repeated in a film in which he played a plagiarist painter: "Inventing a work of art and painting it is easy stuff. What's really difficult is copying!"

But before going any further, something needs to be said about plagiarism and the – not-so-obvious – meaning of the term.

Notes

1 Geller, 2000; Siegrist, 2004; Deazley et al., 2010. Plagiarism is not illegal in the United States in most situations, but it can also result in legal action being taken against the plagiarist, resulting in fines as high as $50,000 and a jail sentence of up to one year.
2 See Borsche (1981).
3 I refer here to the argument of private language developed by Wittgenstein (2001).

Chapter 8

The Freedom of the Slave

It is not futile to refer back to the etymology of the term plagiarism (*plagiat* in French), from the Latin *plagium*. The term referred to a crime, which seemingly consisted of theft of slaves but not physical theft: it applied when someone succeeded in casting such an intense charm on the slave of another that the latter was compelled to submit to them. It was a plagiarism of the mind of someone, to the point not of enslaving them but of making them one's own slave. It effectively denoted what in Haiti they call turning someone into a zombie: a person enslaved not by physical force but through a magical subjugation.

Plagium may come across as a notion miles away from our culture, but that is not necessarily the case. In the 1960s in Italy we incredulously witnessed the "Braibanti Affair".[1] In 1964, at the age of 42, Aldo Braibanti, a communist homosexual poet and former antifascist resistance fighter, had a complaint filed against him by the father of a young friend and lover for *plagio* of his son – who was 23 years old and therefore of legal age – an offence under the fascist legal code, which was still in force at the time: when a person exercises such psychic power over another that they submit them to their will. The young man's father accused Braibanti of subjugating his son, leading him to embrace atheism, communism, homosexuality and literature. He succeeded in having his son locked up in a psychiatric hospital for several months, where he was submitted to electric shocks. Braibanti underwent two trials over a period of four years, and in the second, in 1968, he was sentenced to nine years in prison, of which he served two.

The international press reported on the case, highlighting the anomaly and anachronism of the offence. (It is also remarkable that this crime was foreseen by Fascist law, that is, by a regime that was based on mass "plagiarism" of the Italians by a *Duce*.) In Italy the case sparked a passionate debate – with the political left in favour of abolishing the crime and the right defending it – with the participation of the cream of the Italian intellectuals of the time. The affair led to the abolition of the crime of *plagio* from our criminal code in 1981. The psychiatric violence inflicted on the young man at the behest of his father, with medical complicity, also contributed to the establishment of Law 180 on psychiatric treatment; the 1978 "Basaglia Law", an extremely libertarian law, still in force in Italy, effectively bans

DOI: 10.4324/9781003388098-8

psychiatric hospitals, in the sense that it prohibits doctors from keeping a mentally ill person in a hospital against their will for more than a fortnight.

So, after the Braibanti affair, the term *plagiarized* entered common Italian to refer to someone completely dominated by someone else's mind. It was never used in this "Latin" sense before this affair. But it is interesting to note that the arguments put forward at the time to abolish plagiarism from Italian criminal law were often similar to those used by Lacan to say that plagiarism (as an imitation of someone else's writing) does not exist: that all of us are ultimately plagiarized. By our parents who bring us up, by the teachers who give us an instruction, by our leaders who manipulate us. . . . Our will is mostly the will of the Other, Lacan would say.

Today we consider the father who sued Braibanti a tyrant, precisely because he, the boy's father, never managed to "plagiarize" his own son. He evidently considered him some sort of personal property that another man had taken from him. So, rather than "plagiarizing" his son in turn, he resorted to duress. Today we think the law should have punished the father.

It is interesting to reconstruct how, already in ancient Rome, the term *plagium*, probably very gradually, came to mean what it still means for us: presenting another person's text as one's own. The shift is due to Martial, the Latin satirical poet of the 1st century AD. In his epigrams he repeatedly refers to plagiarists who recited his compositions in public – as was the custom at the time – passing them off as their own or withholding the name of the author. Now the term *plagiarius* in the modern sense appears for the first time in one of his epigrams (Martial, 2015, epigram 52.I) and is more enigmatic than it may appear at first sight:

> I entrust my little books to your care, Quintianus – if I can still call them mine – that your pet poet keeps reciting. If they wail about their intolerable servitude, please be their public defender and stand bail for them; and, when he declares himself their master, please testify that they were mine and I have set them free [*manumissos*]. Proclaim this loudly three or four times and you'll shame the *plagiarist* into keeping quiet [imponem plagiario pudorem].[2]

Martial here talks of his writings as if they were slaves, which another man (probably a certain Fidentinus, with whom he takes issue in other epigrams) has seized by reciting them in public, something which earned Fidentinus the epithet of *plagiarius*. It is interesting to note that Martial does not limit himself to demanding his *libellos*-slaves back with the intercession of Quintianus (probably a lawyer); he says he had freed them, that they were *liberti*. In ancient Rome slaves could become *liberti*, freed by their own owner. In other words, he does not claim the slaves back but accuses the poetaster of enslaving the little books, which were free while they belonged to him. It was necessary, therefore, to restore them to freedom by re-establishing the name of their author. It is as if he were saying: *the author of a text is he who frees these texts*.

There was no printing press at the time, so it must have been quite difficult to protect one's rights as an author. There were no publishers to guarantee the original publication of a work. Works of writing were like banknotes today: the holder is ipso facto their owner. In those days, therefore, plagiarism in the modern sense must have been much more common than today, hence the understandable bitterness of Martial, who was a very popular poet at the time. Moreover, Martial doesn't specify that the poet is trying to pass them off as his own: it was enough for him to read them in public without mentioning that they were the work of Martial.

But what interests us here is the analogy the epigrammatist establishes between writings and slaves. Both involve an uncertain, ambiguous status between object and subject. Slaves, insofar as they belong to someone, are objects, but no one can deny that they are also subjects and therefore belong to themselves and cannot be "plagiarized". The same applies to writings: supposedly they belong to the author, but in fact, insofar as they are made public, they belong to everyone. Yet writings seem to have a subjectivity of their own. It is this public ownership of writings that Martial considers an enslavement. As long as they are attributed to an author, they are free, and therefore made public. But the plagiarist is someone who subjugates them by bringing them to the public himself; he purloins writings.

Elsewhere too, Martial speaks of his writings as objects of trade, just like slaves:

To Fidentinus
A rumour says that you recite
As yours the verses that I write.
Friend, if you'll credit them to me
I'll send you all my poems free;
But if as yours you'd have them known,
Buy them, and they'll become your own.
            (Martial, 2015, epigram 29)

Here Martial seems to suggest something that would be unacceptable to us: selling the authorship of one's writings (but the ghost-writer is today a common figure). We don't know to what extent the suggestion is ironic, but Martial seems to be saying to Fidentinus: "if you want to pass off my writings as your own, you must buy them". Like in a slave market. But the argument is similar to that of the previous epigram: if Fidentinus buys ownership of Martial's texts, he in fact enslaves them, whereas, as long as the authentic author is recognized, the texts are free; they can circulate free of charge.

All this seems very far removed from Lacan's interest in plagiarism. However, as we have seen, like Martial, he also feared he was being plagiarized. But the problematic nature of plagiarism must have raised in him the general question of the *alienation* of the subject in relation to the signifier and also of the letter. If the signifier is only a formal entity, the letter is something material too; however, it is not only material. Like the slave, the letter has a freedom of its own. Ultimately, this is what Lacan has always told us: it is not the human subject who possesses the letters he produces, but it is the letters that subjugate him. Freud said: "The ego is not master in its own house", and Lacan basically said "the subject is not the real master of the letters it produces". Except that letters are by definition public objects – unless you leave your text lying in the drawer. We take it for granted that writings are meant to be read by others even though Lacan would define a piece of writing as *pas-à-lire*, "not to be read" or "passage to reading".

Martial's peculiar thesis is that reciting someone else's verses as if they were your own is a way of enslaving a text that the author had freed, liberated from its latency. But why is a text signed and acknowledged by its author *free*? Plagiarism, in the new (metaphorical) sense it assumed in Martial, does not consist of convincing slaves to change masters but of actually forcing someone to become a slave – not therefore a *servitude volontaire*, as Etienne de la Boétie would call it, but an outright subjugation of texts that were free, or in any case *liberti*.

This strange thesis, however, sheds light on individuals who have the same syndrome as Brain's: those who *can do nothing but plagiarize*. But, unlike Brain, they typically do not even admit to themselves that they are plagiarizing. There are some well-known cases, which I won't mention here. Today people tend to copy and paste from the Internet, but before the Internet, they would copy directly from other texts. And usually these plagiarists do not recognize themselves as such.

The reverse case is those who are convinced that they're always being plagiarized. If by any chance they meet a particular author one day and then read the book later published by this author, they become convinced that the author stole their ideas or expressions. This is often the case when couples, women and men, and even of two women or two men, publish a book together: it sometimes leads to conflicts that may even lead to separation or divorce. At least one of the two thinks they've been intellectually "robbed" by the other. This recalls paranoid behaviour: one is certain of having fallen victim to the other, who was until recently perceived as a sort of ideal twin. Persecution here takes the form of "s/he stole my ideas!" But even when the supposed plagiarist is not one's partner in a couple, the appropriation by the "great writer" is experienced as persecutory: the powerful exploit "those like me who count for nothing", the same way as capitalists are considered to exploit workers. We have just said that Prof. Brain's modality of plagiarism is a melancholic one: it is not the other who plagiarizes me, it is I who plagiarizes the other; I am the guilty party.

Both compulsive non-confessing plagiarists and those who often feel paranoically plagiarized deny reality, albeit in inverse forms: the former do not recognize that their ideas and texts actually belong to the *other*; the latter do not recognize that the *other's* ideas do not belong to them. They're both in a psychotic mode, whereas Professor Brain is in a purely neurotic mode: he fears that his thoughts are those of others, but this fear prevents him from writing what he thinks.

Plagiarism is not simply a matter, as one might think, of stealing from the other something that the other has and flaunting one's feathers but of a misappropriation that deprives the text of its freedom, because developing original ideas is equivalent to *setting ideas free*. It is as if ideas had always pre-existed but in a state of latency, of imprisonment, I would say, and those who write them down give them not only visibility but the freedom to express themselves. Indeed, many authors claim that through their novels *the things themselves* come forward, almost begging to be revealed. So, landscapes, characters and ideas come essentially from *outside the writer* and use the author as a medium to manifest themselves. As Picasso used to say, "I don't look for, I find". Note: not "I don't look for, I invent". Artists always *find* outside themselves what they will represent, freeing it from latency.

In the preface to *Six Characters in Search of an Author*, Luigi Pirandello (1921) describes the six characters as beings coming to meet him, asking, almost imploring the author to transfer them to writing. Analogously, ideas are "Platonic", in the sense that they are not in our mind, in the same way that circles, squares or rectangles are not in our mind. All our mind does is *recognize them*. Ideas are like Michelangelo's *Prisoners*, who still appear trapped in the stone from which they are struggling to extricate themselves, in constant danger of being sucked back into the marble from which the sculptor has freed their forms (and this is how Michelangelo himself described his work as a sculptor: a *freeing of forms* from their marble prisons).

Conceiving ideas and putting them down on paper is an act of freedom, but for many the temptation to subjugate them, to exploit them for personal éclat, is too strong. Plagiarists know that these ideas were not their own, but their pleasure comes from manifesting them as such, in this way curbing their freedom. Plagiarism is equivalent to purloining letters. Because it's true that ideas are not other people's, but from the moment that they are stolen, passed off as one's own, then they really become *other* from what they are. Paradoxically, plagiarism confers an intellectual property that had previously been unnecessary.

If in our unconscious writing something happens exactly as Martial describes it – an act of liberation that plagiarism can reverse – this can perhaps help us understand a few more things about Professor Brain. He didn't wish to *deliver ideas*: if he delivered them, he would be convinced that he was subjugating them. (The English *to deliver* comes etymologically from the old French *delivrer*, which in turn comes from the Latin *de-liberare*, to free from.) In a dream of his, in which he is fighting his father, they use books instead of weapons, and when one of the two seizes the other's book, he swallows it. Now, a book serves a purpose if you can go through the pages, but in this case the books are devoured, destroyed. What emerges, in short, is a destructive intent towards the ideas of others. In the same way, plagiarism reveals an intent to destroy the ideas of others (the other's penis?). Decorating oneself with other people's jewellery is only one phase of the plagiaristic syndrome; at the core, there is a will to destroy these jewels. The basis is always a rivalry; one copies a rival, admired precisely insofar as fantasized as "better than me". So plagiarism is not only appropriation: it is a destruction of ideas. Or rather, the destruction of their freedom, insofar as someone has liberated them.

When in 1956 Lacan published Kris's case, he was 55 years old and hadn't published much until then. The only work of his that had been printed was his doctorate thesis on paranoia (Lacan (1975 [1933]), as well as the entry for *Family* (Lacan,

2003) in the *Encyclopédie Française* and a few articles and papers: very little for a tremendously ambitious man like Lacan. Did he have problems publishing, just like Prof. Brain? Perhaps, but he certainly had an ethical and theoretical problem with writing and publishing.

Lacan never personally published his *Écrits* nor his *Seminars*, both compiled by his son-in-law Jacques-Alain Miller. Even when he was still alive, the published Seminars were all transcribed and edited by Miller. He sometimes referred to "publishing" as *poubellication*, from *poubelle*, waste-paper basket or trash. He evidently had resistance to publishing his works in volumes, something which points to the more general, and to him central, question of the *letter*.

Everything leads us to think that ultimately Lacan resisted publishing his writings and seminars because he thought that by feeding them to the public, they would become estranged. Not from him, but they would become estranged *tout court*. That, once read, his writings would become enslaved. This partly explains his cryptic style, the effort somehow to encipher his writings, make them unintelligible, ensure that others would not take them with them, together with them: he thought that understanding them was somehow equivalent to taking possession of them, absorbing them, "devouring" them, as Prof. Brain did unconsciously. Brain did not complain about stealing other people's letters but the meaning of what they said – and Lacan has a point when he says that the sense of the letters does not belong to anyone in particular – as the law regulating copyright also states. Yet, as in the dream in which he uses books as weapons (Kris, 1951, p. 23), Brain treats texts as edible. Texts are at once food and subjective thoughts. For him stealing is devouring. But this must have resonated for Lacan, in the sense that the alienation of letters can be accomplished through the propagation of sense. Lacan's wanting to obscure meaning was his way of defending his writings from the subjugation that every publication, every making public, every circulation among the public, implies. Lacan wished to keep his letters *free*.

When in 1968 Lacan began editing the journal of his école, *Scilicet* – of which only five issues were published – he decided that the contributors would publish their texts anonymously. Only he, Lacan, would sign his contributions with his initials. Should this be put on the tally of Lacan's despotic inclinations? Probably. But beyond the narcissistic radicalism of Lacan as a man, there remains his urge – consistent with that era of abstract Marx-Leninist fury – to establish a sort of collective thinking that would bypass an individualistic property of ideas, not unlike the famous group of French mathematicians known as Bourbaki, who signed all their works only with the invented name Nicolas Bourbaki. In a certain sense Lacan wanted all his students to sign their contributions with the name "Lacan"; he wanted the name Lacan, like Bourbaki, to be the unifying signifier. But perhaps the signature "Lacan", like "Bourbaki", is the signature of nobody. Lacan's collectivist ideal– even if limited to a system of thought – is an aspect we will not have time to delve into here, but it does shed light on many historical events in the Lacanian movement after his death: the need to sign oneself as "Lacan-thought", the same way Maoists once spoke of "Mao-thought". (Both his daughter Judith and his

son-in-law Jacques-Alain Miller were Maoist militants in a Maoist organization
called Gauche prolétarienne in the 1970s.)

Lacan certainly suffered a contradiction in the flesh, I would say. On the one
hand is his idea that there is no such thing as a plagiarism of thoughts, on the other
his need for an extreme individualization. Not surprisingly, his style is absolutely
personal, inimitable and unique. If you happen to read two lines by Lacan, you immediately say "This is Lacan!" Every contradiction can be "put into perspective"
by dialectical thinking, true. But in a dialectics with no synthesis – like Lacan's –
contradiction remains contradiction, no *Aufhebung*; it does not elevate itself, and
it is not evaded. How to reconcile the principle according to which "the unconscious is the thought of the Other" – and therefore that which is the most intimate
thing about me does not belong to me – and his idiosyncratic passion for his own
uniqueness?

Notes

1 This affair has recently become popular again in Italy after the release of the movie *Il
signore delle formiche* (The Lord of the Ants) by Gianni Amelio in 2022.
2 Commendo tibi, Quintiane, nostros – /Nostros dicere si tamen libellos/Possum, quos
recitat tuus poeta–:/Si de servitio gravi queruntur,/Adsertor venias satisque praestes,/Et,
cum se dominum vocabit ille,/Dicas esse meos manuque missos./Hoc si terque quaterque
clamitaris,/Inpones plagiario pudorem.

Chapter 9

Statement and Enunciation

I have highlighted and commented on Lacan's distortions in relation to Kris's text, as others have done before me, not to discredit Lacan. Rather, what interests me here is Lacan's unconscious: *misreading*, as Harold Bloom calls it, is a formation of the unconscious, to use Lacan's own terms.

Interpreting a text, and not only in a psychoanalytical key, means separating two levels that Lacan himself distinguished following the linguist Émile Benveniste (1966, 1974): the level of *statements* (*énoncés*) and that of *enunciations* (*énonciations*). In fact, interpreting the unconscious means to shift from the level of statements to that of enunciations. Enunciations are quite similar to what John Austin has called performative language.

A statement is the totality of words spoken that form an explicit proposition and which lends itself to syntactic and formal analysis. An enunciation is the act that gives the background sense – mainly intersubjective – of a statement that can never be ignored in concrete life. Stopping at statements – at the "letter" – would mean not understanding anything about the living, active, signification of discourse. Enunciations are the *acting* of speech.

A common joke in America today: "In New York they say 'fuck you' to mean 'I love you'; in California they say 'I love you' to mean 'fuck you!'". This is a good illustration of how often a statement can reverse the meaning of an enunciation and vice versa.

Freud (1905a) told the famous story of the two Jews meeting on a train in Galicia. A asks B where he's going and the latter replies: "To Cracow". A replies: "Why are you telling me you're going to Cracow to have me believe you're going to Lemberg, while you really are going to Cracow?" B's answer "I'm going to Cracow" is the statement, whereas A's reactions illustrate the complexity of the enunciation.

These texts by Kris and Lacan should also be read as enunciative acts. In philosophy of language (Austin, 1962), enunciative acts are known as *performative speech*, which amount to doing things with words. If I say "I promise I'll come and see you", I am not only saying I will come and see you, but I am also acting out a promise. And in fact, if I fail to keep it, I could be reprimanded. Psychoanalysis in general owes its effectiveness to this performative dimension of language, to the fact that speaking also amounts to acting.

DOI: 10.4324/9781003388098-9

As Alessandra Campo (2020) pointed out, acting out in psychoanalysis is the reverse of a performative act: if the latter amounts to saying something that has the sense of an authentic social act, instead acting out is an act which, for the analyst, has the sense of a saying, of a message sent to the analyst. Performative enunciation is a saying that results in an act; acting out is an action that results in a saying.

Now, the publication by Kris of this case was itself an acting out, in an undoubtedly aggressive sense. Kris actually writes that the patient wished not to have his first analyst, Schmideberg, know he'd resumed analysis with someone else. By publishing this case in an important journal, one Schmideberg most likely read, Kris is evidently by no means respectful of his patient's wishes (or had these wishes changed in the meantime?). In addition, he also ensures that every reader will recognize Schmideberg as Brain's first analyst! So, by publishing the case not only does Kris says to his colleague something that he'd promised to his patient not to let her know, but he also informs his colleagues around the world about it. And though Kris doesn't openly criticize the first analysis, he does in fact show its limitations as an outdated analysis. We can imagine that his patient flew into a rage when he saw his case described publicly in this way. Was Kris's publication itself a counter-transferential act?

One also wonders why Kris, among the various things he could have said about his relation with the patient, chose to reveal something so embarrassing: his broken covenant with Brain not to inform his previous analyst. By revealing the name of his predecessor, he is also "telling" us how worthless his promises are. Kris probably exposed himself to this general reprimand because *it was very important for him* not only to inform his colleague how much better than her he had been but also to inform everyone how he had been a better analyst than Melitta, since she had failed, at least to some extent.

In other words, publishing those notes was a political act against his colleague, who was also living in New York at the time. Instead of *speaking against* her, Kris *acted out* his disapproval.

Why such an evident attack by Kris on his colleague? It's worth illustrating what Schmideberg and Kris's positions were in the psychoanalytic movement of the time.

Melitta (1904–1983) was the daughter of Melanie and Arthur Klein. Melanie had analysed her three young children, including Melitta, on whose case she wrote an article in 1923 (Klein, 1924), calling her Lisa, an eighteen-year-old girl. Analysing one's own child was common practice at the time. Freud had said that only a parent is capable of analysing a child (Freud, 1909a) and himself analysed his daughter Anna. "Like Freud, Klein tried to turn her children into followers and followers into her children" (Turkle, 1986).

Analysed from an early age, Melitta was encouraged by her mother to attend meetings of the Psychoanalytic Society in Budapest, where Melanie had been living since the age of fifteen. Melitta devoured psychoanalytic literature and soon began practicing as an analyst herself. She underwent five personal analyses in addition to that with her mother (with Max Eitingon, Karen Horney, Hanns Sachs, Ella Sharpe and Edward Glover), and she married a psychoanalyst she'd met in Berlin, Walter Schmideberg, who died in 1954 of complications related to alcohol abuse.

In 1935 a dramatic, unrelenting conflict between the two women began. Melitta later claimed that her mother had always hated her, a hatred that she cordially reciprocated. The conflict took the form of Melitta's frontal opposition to Kleinian theories, which mother Klein upheld steadfastly, imposing total loyalty on her followers somewhat despotically. Backed by Edward Glover, who loathed Klein, Melitta launched an unprecedented war against her mother's theories. At meetings of the British Psychoanalytic Society (BPS), Melitta would rant at length against Melanie's ideas while her mother listened in silence to the attacks. Klein told people that her daughter was psychotic (at the time the theory that people become psychotic if they didn't have a mother good enough, in short, that parents are essentially responsible for the psychosis of their children, had not yet become a cliché among analysts).

It is also interesting to note that in 1936, Schmideberg – two years after publishing her essay in which she speaks of the plagiarist – reported six authors of the Kleinian school to the Education Committee of the BPS for plagiarism in certain parts of their book. This was a volume edited by John Rickman, *On the Bringing up of Children*, with contributions by Ella Sharpe, Nina Searl, Merrell Middlemore and Susan Isaacs. But the allegations of plagiarism were not validated (Grosskurth, 1986).

The mother–daughter conflict was just one aspect of a period known as the Great Controversies, when there was a violent confrontation between the theses of Anna Freud and of her supporters – which were supposed to be orthodox, in line with Sigmund Freud – and those of Klein and her supporters, who were mostly female (see King and Steiner, 1991). The debates were so heated during the war that sometimes the BPS analysts didn't even notice the sirens announcing air raids over London.[1] Melitta was not at all an Anna-Freudian (on the contrary, she'd attacked Anna Freud even before attacking her mother [Schmideberg, 1935]), but in fact she furthered the latter's cause with the ferocity of her criticism of her mother's works (personally, I find much of that criticism quite cogent; sometimes hatred makes us quite clear headed).

In 1945, Melitta emigrated to the United States, where she reconnected with psychoanalyst friends from her Berlin youth. Disillusioned with the New York psychoanalytic milieux too (and hence also with Ernst Kris, I presume), she gradually abandoned psychoanalysis and turned to other psychotherapies. She focused on the analysis and treatment of teenage delinquents, emphasizing family and environmental factors (as chance would have it! After all, she too had been a "delinquent" daughter in her mother's eyes). Basically, in time she broke away from the psychoanalytic imprinting imposed on her by her mother. Up until the very end she condemned her mother's analytic practice "too active" (I would have said exactly the same).

In 1963 she resigned from the BPS and stopped engaging with the analytic milieux of London and New York, both of which had sickened her. She never reconciled with her mother and continued to refuse to speak to her. She didn't even attend Melanie's funeral, even though she was in London. "On the day of her memorial service, her daughter Melitta delivered a final posthumous insult by giving a professional lecture wearing flamboyant red boots".[2]

Kris's ungracious acting out with Schmideberg is explained by the fact that at the time of her publication (1934) she was still "Kleinian", so it was an indirect way of attacking her mother. And he'd probably found out about Melitta's tendency to break away from psychoanalysis and seek inspiration in other forms of psychotherapy. In short, Melitta was a reprobate even for ego psychologists.

Notes

1 "The on-going debate about the true nature and origins of the infant's psychological life was so fierce that its participants hardly noticed that London was about to be bombed. Amidst the storm of words, D.W. Winnicott calmly stood up and said: 'I should like to point out that there is an air raid going on'". Grosskurth (1986), p. 321.
2 Grosskurth (1986). Also Roudinesco and Plon (1997).

Chapter 10

French Controversies

Understanding Lacan's commentary, however, also means grasping its performative enunciation beyond his explicit statements. And to understand Lacan's utterances in this case, we need to consider Lacan's situation in relation to the institutional framework of psychoanalysis at the time.

In 1953 a major split had taken place in French psychoanalysis. Many analysts – including Lacan and his friend and supporter Françoise Dolto – had left the Société Psychanalytique de Paris (SPP) and founded a new Société Française de Psychanalyse (SFP), led by Daniel Lagache, a university professor whose core ideas were very different from those of Lacan and Dolto. In short, it was a political alliance and, as such, an opportunistic one. By leaving the SPP, however, the SFP also excluded itself from the International Psychoanalytic Association (IPA), founded by Freud and still today the leading psychoanalytic association in the world. At the time no analyst who had joined the SFP, including Lacan and Dolto, had the slightest intention of leaving the IPA: anyone who wanted to be recognized as a real psychoanalyst had to be a member. So, a series of negotiations and *pourparlers* that would go on for ten years followed.

In 1963 the SFP was readmitted to the IPA, but the latter demanded that Lacan and Dolto have their right of training psychoanalysts taken away from them. At the time IPA analysts were not concerned with Lacan's ideas as such; they were only worried about the fact that Lacan's sessions were variable in time and did not stick to the standard 45–50 minutes (a criterion based on the fact that this was the duration of Freud's sessions). Everyone knew that this variable time basically resulted in shorter sessions of around twenty minutes or less. In the eyes of the IPA leaders, this was intolerable. In any case, neither Lacan nor Dolto could accept the diktat of being excluded as trainers, so Lacan founded a new association, the École Freudienne de Paris, of which Dolto became a pivotal member. The latter existed until 1980, when Lacan, a year before his death, dissolved it.

When Lacan spoke or wrote the texts we are discussing here (in 1954, 1956 and 1958), he was therefore waiting to be co-opted by the IPA after the split. And since he was criticized above all for his analytical technique, it's hardly surprising that he opened his seminar with *The Technical Writings of Freud*, as if to reaffirm his basic continuity with Freud's inspiration at the clinical level too. It's also interesting

DOI: 10.4324/9781003388098-10

to point out that almost all of Lacan's writings dealing with questions of analytic technique are situated in this period, between 1953 and 1963, precisely when his practice was being challenged and investigated. Once he'd created his own school, Lacan would no longer return to technical questions.

What is surprising, however, is that instead of lying low in those years, Lacan not only attacked the practice of Kris –an eminent IPA figure – but, as we shall see, even that of Anna Freud, considered at the time the true heir of Sigmund's thought. It's as if in that period Lacan had been inviting the IPA to expel him.

Shortly afterwards he would also openly criticize the ideas of Daniel Lagache, a member of his same psychoanalytical association.[1] At the time Lacan seemed to be shaken by a dangerous controversial zeal, which was to diminish in time.

In his 1954 seminar Lacan took sides with Melanie Klein. The rift in Great Britain was even more dramatic than in France, as we said. It's worth noting that both Anna Freud and Melanie Klein were German speaking and had emigrated to England. Anna Freud's followers were referred to as "Freudians", taking for granted that Sigmund and Anna were part of the same Freudianism. Klein's followers were known as Kleinians. When I went to Britain in the 1970s, the BPS was divided into three structures, each with a different form of training: the Freudians (those following the line of Anna Freud), the Kleinians and the Independents (Winnicott, Bion and many others) – all members of the same Society, but deeply divided. I arrived from France, where calling yourself a "Freudian" meant either being a Lacanian or in any case a Freudian very far moved from the theses of Anna Freud. So at the time I found those English labels quite bizarre.

Lacan's attack on Kris, therefore, had a precise political sense: it was a way of openly siding with the "English", or Kleinian, school against the "American", which had remained faithful to Anna Freud. In the background then, as we shall see more clearly further on, the sense of an enunciation emerges: "The true heirs of Freud are not those who claim they are".

Note

1 See Jacques Lacan, "Remarks on Daniel Lagache's presentation: 'Psychoanalysis and personality structure'", in *E I*, Ecrits, pp. 543–574.

Chapter 11

The Missing Name

A few lines earlier, Lacan had Kris address his patient as follows:

> "Only the ideas of others are truly interesting, they're the only ones one can take; the taking is a question of know-how [*s'en emparer est une question de savoir s'y prendre*]" – this is how I have chosen to translate *engineering* [In English in the original], because I think it echoes the famous American *how-to* [In English in the original].[1]

> (*Écrits*, p. 331)

Kris, however, wrote:

> Only the ideas of others were truly interesting, only ideas one could take; hence the taking had to be engineered.

The term used by Kris is *engineered*, not *engineering*. It is not the same thing.[2]

To *engineer* means to obtain with machinations but also to plan out something that will be implemented. In French it could be translated as: "*il fallait donc s'évertuer à [se débrouiller pour] s'en emparer*". All Kris is saying is that the subject is contriving the methods for acquiring the only ideas that are of any value to him: other people's ideas. But then why this further distortion of Kris's text by Lacan?

On the one hand here Lacan presents as active (*engineering*) something that was in the passive (*engineered*); on the other he portrays as a talent something that Kris instead denotes as a neurotic scraping along. Here Kris is alluding to the fact that, since the ideas of others are the only ones of any interest to Brain, he can only use his own ideas if they appear to belong to others.

Indeed, this misreading allows Lacan to point his finger at what seems to him the fundamental ethical flaw of ego psychology: thinking of intersubjectivity in mercantilist terms, in those of a liberal economy, as a give and take. And he goes so far as to say that Kris makes his patient come across as an obsessional neurotic (but Kris doesn't issue any kind of diagnosis). What Lacan seeks to condemn here is the fact that Kris ascribes to his patient a "give and have" mechanism (the text actually

DOI: 10.4324/9781003388098-11

says "give and take"). According to Lacan, Kris sees an obsessional structure in the patient: "We should not, of course, disdain the making conscious of an obsessional symptom, but it is something else altogether to fabricate such a symptom from scratch" (*Écrits*, p. 330), Lacan laments. If Kris reads an obsessional problem in Prof. Brain, this is because, Lacan insinuates, the Austrian Kris has entered the American obsessive mentality, in which every relationship is based on a *quid pro quo*, and what counts is the balance between giving and taking. According to Lacan, the capitalist world – "capitalist discourse", as he would later call it – is inherently obsessional.

But, if it's true that Brain was of German origin and living in London, the argument does not hold at all.

Lacan then evokes the concept of *bilanisme* – from *bilan*, maintaining equipoise, balance sheet; the English translation, "summaryism", is unsuitable. Oddly enough, he doesn't quote the name of the analyst who developed the notion. About him he merely says that he is "one of my early and sorely missed teachers and masters, whose every twist and turn in thought I did not follow for all that". Who was this "early master" of Lacan?

He was the Swiss psychoanalyst Charles Odier (1886–1954), who died on 28 July 1954, a few months after Lacan's first seminar, a death that therefore precedes the publication of Lacan's text by around two years. If Odier had been one of his teachers and masters, quoting his name could have been a way of paying a posthumous tribute to him. But he does not. What prevented Lacan from writing an obituary and ensuring that the name of a teacher whom he said that he sorely missed was visible in print? Is there something like a grudge between the two in the background?

Even when we *fail to state* something – in this case the name of the friend and teacher – this lack in the statement fills the enunciation with meaning. If quoting someone is an act, not quoting them is an act also. Those who publish know only too well how many enemies they can make simply by forgetting to quote in one of their books or papers the writings of friends they say are among their closest and dearest! *Not quoting* someone is often a lack crying out from the pages of a book. Kris acted against his patient and against Schmideberg by publishing that case and publishing the name of the latter, but Lacan too acted by not publishing Odier's name. Can it be a coincidence that texts revolving around an acting are in many ways acting outs in themselves?

But, as we saw, interpreting Brain's gluttony as an acting out is improper. The maze is becoming more and more intricate.

Notes

1 Jacques Lacan, "Response to Jean Hyppolite's Commentary on Freud's 'Verneinung'" (this, however, is my own translation from the French).
2 Fink (2004) omits the second part of Lacan's sentence ("*je traduis ainsi: engineering, parce que je pense qu'il fait écho au célèbre* how to *américain, mettons, si ce n'est pas*

ça: question de planification") in quoting it and in the footnote: "(397.3) Lacan provides a comment here (which I have omitted) on the English term 'engineering', suggesting that it is related to the famous American 'how to', or, if not, to the notion of planning (discussed in the last section of Kris's article). He seems, however, not to understand the meaning of the verb form, 'to engineer', as used here, for the translation he provides is "*s'en emparer reste une question de savoir s'y prendre*" (taking it is a matter of knowing how to go about it).

Chapter 12

... *Perseverare Diabolicum Est*

It is truly extraordinary how Lacan, in the subsequent references to Brain's case, completely forgets his corrections of 1956 and, as if by a sort of inertia, goes back to his previous version.

In the seminar of 23 January 1963, dedicated essentially to the distinction between *passage à l'act*e (passage to the act) and acting out, he says:

> Kris seeks to silence his patient by means of the truth. He shows him in the most irrefutable way that he is not a plagiarist, he has read his book and it is well and truly original. On the contrary, the others are the ones who've been copying him. The subject cannot dispute this. Only, he doesn't give a damn. And when he leaves, what does he go and do? As you know . . . he goes and gobbles down [*bouffer*] a plate of fresh brains.
>
> . . . I'm teaching you to recognize acting-out and what it means, namely, what I'm designating for you as the *a* or the pound of flesh.
>
> With the fresh brains, the patient simply signals something to Ernst Kris. *Everything you say is true, only it leaves the question unscathed. There are still fresh brains. To make a point of it, I'm going to eat some right afterwards so that I can tell you about it in the next session.*
>
> (*Sem* 10, pp. 124–125)

It is surprising how in a few lines Lacan commits a long series of errors concerning Kris's text, errors that we have already illustrated. By now, this anecdote of the fresh brains has become for Lacan the prototypical example of an acting out, and as such, it will be passed on to the Lacanian schools. This distortion is in fact now an integral part of the transmission of Lacanian doctrine in universities as well.

But this is not at all an exception in cultural fields. For instance, I often hear philosophers and anthropologists say "Eskimos have many words for various kinds of snow, but no single term or concept for 'snow'", to illustrate the philosophical important theory of incommensurability between tongues – a fact which unfortunately is false.[1] Sometimes I have the feeling that most of the beliefs, even of intellectuals, which most texts or speeches take for granted are based on rumours, urban legends, fake news, myths.

DOI: 10.4324/9781003388098-12

Needless to say, all of this electrifies Lacan bashers. However, it would be possible to do nit-picking with many other important authors, almost all of them. Starting with Freud – by now we know all the quotations he got wrong, all his contradictions, the sentences that cast others in a bad light, his prejudices and so on.

The best-known and most-quoted misquotation is that of *Leonardo da Vinci and a Memory of His Childhood*, which Freud (1910) considered one of his most beautiful texts. Freud develops a complex theory on the personality and partly on the art of Leonardo starting from a childhood memory in which a vulture (*Geier* in German) slams its tail into the mouth of the little Leonardo. However, Freud had read about this memory in a bad German translation, where the word vulture was used to translate what was, in Italian, a kite (*nibbio*). This detail brings down his entire, certainly ingenious, analytic construction about Leonardo. And what is even more disturbing is that Freud, republishing his text several times, does not take into account the correction made in 1923 by an English historian of the Renaissance, Eric MacLagan (1923). We could make a very long list, in fact, of the ineffectiveness of corrections in the history of culture: for centuries errors that had been demonstrated as such early on continue to be repeated.[2]

However, the case of the man that eats fresh brains seems to be more serious because Lacan, as we have said, repeats a mistake that he himself had in some way corrected. Now, as we all know, this persevering in error happens to everyone, and all the time. Telling the truth in most cases doesn't help: when the other person "gets an idea into his head, it's hard to get it out of there", as the saying goes. In short, the human critical spirit is quite limited, even among the most rigorous intellectuals.

Among the millions of anecdotes I could tell, I will limit myself to one taken from my own experience. Years ago, a dear friend of mine, a cultured and intelligent woman, in a discussion among friends, made a major accusation against the Catholic Church, which, according to her, was, by prohibiting the use of condoms, in fact partly responsible for an increase of population, particularly in the countries known as "developing". It was very common to show such rancour against Catholicism at the time. As it happens, however, I was familiar with the topic of birth control because I have worked on this very issue. I pointed out to her – citing the main bibliography – that the fertility of nations is only very weakly correlated with religious belief. Demographers agree that what counts is the economic and industrial development of a country: the more developed a country is, the fewer children are born. As a result, Catholic Italy has a very low fertility rate, while Protestant, Muslim and tribal African countries have a very high fertility rate. The Catholic Church is not responsible for the global population increase. My friend, an intelligent and spirited person, admitted that I was right.

To my great surprise, one year later, at a dinner party my friend came up with exactly the same tirade against the Catholic Church, responsible for a birth rate out of control. . . . In short, it was as if I had spoken to a wall. My friend had forgotten that she had already been "convinced" otherwise.

I know that I, like everyone else, do not learn from my human mistakes; rather I persevere, like everyone else, diabolically. Nor do I escape what I would call the glue of belief, and I know how much my awareness of being stuck myself is paradoxical, like the Cretan Epimenides, who said that all Cretans are liars.

What is it that makes certain beliefs, of whatever kind, become so stubbornly stuck in our minds and resist all correction? A psychoanalyst obviously tends to give profound explanations; that is, what comes into play is something Lacan himself called "unconscious knowledge". For example, for my friend, the subject of fertility was not an indifferent one: she had never had children, and later in life suffered a lot because of this.

Today, thanks to historians of science, we know that the same thing happens with the transmission of scientific ideas. That is, the idealized image we have of scientists as champions of critical sense, ready to give up their own theory if it is proved wrong, hardly reflects reality. (This is what the historical reconstructions of scientific knowledge by Paul Feyerabend show.) Max Planck said that a new scientific theory, especially if it is revolutionary, eventually prevails not because it convinces all scientists in a certain field, but simply because the avid supporters of the old theory retire or die, and their place is taken by young people now trained in the new ideas.

This may lead us to moderately sceptical conclusions: it is by no means enough to bring overwhelming evidence to support a certain idea and convince others, even when these others are very rational minds. The unconscious entrenchment of our ideas mostly proves stronger. Nothing is more difficult than persuading someone who has no intention of being persuaded. And I know very well that not even this book will persuade a convinced Lacanian of the limits of Lacan's thought and knowledge; he or she will always end up finding good reasons to justify Lacan's errors. Nor will it ever persuade an anti-Lacanian, who is convinced that Lacan is a charlatan and a peddler of snake oil and disregard the possibility that, despite his errors and distortions, he ends up by offering insights that we need to address.

Hence the question that I shall not answer: what is the point of writing and publishing?

As for Lacan's obstinacy in seeing Brain's case as an exemplary case of acting out, we should, in this sense, question his unconscious motivation. Dealing with this topic, there must have been a fundamental identification with this subject, as Kris describes him. He too, after all, had great problems publishing (his *Écrits* would perhaps never have been published if Jacques-Alain Miller had not edited them), and it is evident that his immense culture, his wanting to cover the most diverse and disparate fields, must have been the effect of a fantastic oral drive to eat all the "great brains" in Western history. He must have seen this devouring of other people's books as his own acting out.

Notes

1 On this "great Eskimo vocabulary Hoax": Martin, 1986; Pullum, 1991; Pinker, 1994, p. 64.

2 The most dramatic and historically influencing hoax is the fabrication of *The Protocol of the Elders of Sion* (1903), which was discovered to be completely false in 1921: it was taken as a true text by Nazi and fascist propaganda and is taken to be a real document by millions of people even today, officially by some anti-Israeli movements like Hamas. It was endorsed as true by many Arab leaders like Nasser and Sadat in Egypt, al-Gaddafi in Libya, the Palestinian Solidarity Committee . . .

Chapter 13

Understanding Is Misunderstanding

The fact that Lacan does not remain faithful to his own corrections but falls back – as someone may fall back into an old vice – into the distorted version that he obviously prefers opens up a huge question, and not only in psychoanalysis. This is no less than the question of the transmission of a certain knowledge, as well as of a knowhow. This is the question Plato had already addressed in his *Meno*: is it possible to teach, that is, to transmit, the *areté*? In Greek the word meant "ability", "skill", "talent".

How can the psychoanalytic *areté* be transmitted? This is the question at the heart of all psychoanalytic institutions and schools, and it produces divergences, splits . . . not incidentally, because the question is still unresolved. And it points to an even more general and fundamental problem: what does it mean to transmit knowledge and skill? But we will not delve into this vast issue. The point is: how can it happen that Lacan transmits wrongly to himself?

Classical social psychology studies of the transmission of information almost all conclude that transmission between individuals is like individual memory, which is a form of transmission of recollections to oneself: it inevitably distorts the original information. The lines of distortion have been described both in memory and transmission. Here we will consider only two: *narrative consonance* and *simplification*, studied in particular by F.C. Bartlett in the 1930s. Bartlett (1932) distributed a number of texts from cultures far removed from the British among Cambridge students. The first to have read the text would describe it to a second and the second to a third, and so on . . . by the end of the process, he could see what the initial story had become. These were Cambridge students, and thus young people who scored highly in intellectual abilities. The results were that the initial texts were drastically distorted.

For example, Bartlett had distributed a Native American tale full of mystical symbolism and cultural references foreign to English culture. The final output was a rather trite story with a very British feel. The narrative was gradually stripped of its cultural exoticisms and its ambiguous features and became increasingly conventional and predictable. For example, the original text read: "When the sun rose, he fell to the ground. Something black came out of his mouth. His face contracted". This is a complex experience that alludes to spiritual experiences and magical

DOI: 10.4324/9781003388098-13

beliefs. Through transmission from person to person, the strange black thing became the soul that leaves the body, and eventually we arrive at this version: "His spirit left the world".

If this happens with Amerindian tales, we can imagine what complex doctrines such as Freud's or Lacan's must undergo! Sooner or later, we shall inexorably find ourselves with a smoothed-over vulgate. And even if some scholars are then scrupulous enough to return to the original texts, often the vulgate in which they are steeped will act so as to filter their direct reading: in Freud's or Lacan's texts, they will always read what the orthodoxy of their own school makes them see. This is what we can call *narrative consonance*: what matters is for a fact to fit into the "correct narrative" that describes the world. All elements need to fit into the pre-established schema. (I modify here the term *cognitive consonance* advanced by Leon Festinger, 1957.) What matters is for a fact to fit into the "correct narrative" that describes the world unless the scholar in question is a particularly scrupulous, restless, critical, in short a rather neurotic, spirit.

This simplification ready for mass transmission – consistent with the official theory – also occurs with Lacan's various interventions on Professor Brain.

For example, a prestigious leader of a Lacanian institute wrote:

At one point, when his patient complains about the fact that he copies everything, Kris pulls out a book from the library and shows him, proof in hand, that he has copied nothing. The patient accepts this and – a famous episode – goes to eat something after the session: fresh brains.

(Laurent, 1989)

In fact, this version – completely erroneous, as we have shown – is what thousands of Lacanians of the various schools learn in their training. But this is no one's fault, nor is there any bad faith at the source; it is the very logic of transmission as studied by social psychologists.

In general, whatever is complex is gradually reduced, simplified, often trivialized. And what appears strange, foreign, unexpected is brought back to the familiar, the already known, the expected. In information theory it is said that a loss of information occurs. In Lacanian terms we would say: the ego (of the second topic) "imaginarizes" the real. To transmit is to de-realize; it is to fit what doesn't square with the expected patterns into the regular pattern. The human being, through memory, interpretation and transmission, transforms the real world into a fairy-tale, as Nietzsche (1888) said. And always into the same monotonous fairy-tale.

Now we can speak of distortions because we have a fixed point of comparison. The experimenter is in possession of the original text, which has remained unchanged, and can therefore compare the various versions and judge them to be distorted. We are allowed to say that Lacan distorts Kris's text because we have the original. But in real life we mostly lack this fixed point. Even when we do have texts, no one can issue the sole authoritative interpretation of these texts. We have

Kant's and Freud's texts, but we don't have a setting with the correct interpretation that allows us to say with certainty: "This reading misunderstands Kant, misunderstands Freud!" Not least because they are dead authors.

Some more restless spirits attack the simplifications of any school, be it philosophical, psychoanalytical, political and so on. These spirits are disgusted by the fabulation of the world, which is, however, inescapable. Culture is a machine that constantly reduces complexity. There are certain moments when revolutions of the mind are set in motion in a culture, and simplifications are swept aside for a moment. Great authors move us by putting us in contact with shreds of the real. But the simplifying and ego-centralizing machine soon comes into action: it makes sure that any patch of the real is gradually absorbed by simplification and the familiar. This absorption is the task of schools, universities, academies, encyclopaedias, academic curricula and so on. They all ensure that the hurricanes of the real are extinguished in the calm lake of common sense.

This is also what happens to Lacan with regard to the texts he discusses. We could say that when Lacan talks about Professor Brain, he simplifies himself. He fails to transmit correctly to himself. He relates the case to what he believes *acting out* to be: a way of saying to the analyst "I couldn't give a damn about your attempt to recall me to reality!"

But if that was what Lacan was keen to say, why did he rely on someone else's case? And why did he distort it? What did Lacan want to say to himself that he failed to say to his readers?

In fact, he chose a case in which the analyst does not call the analysand back to reality but to something far more complex: to the relation between a subject and his signifiers. To say "maybe you never plagiarized" is not the same as saying "you believe you raped a little girl, but you didn't". (I am thinking about a psychotic man who was convinced he had raped his niece when she was four years old, even if he had absolutely no memory of the supposed rape and the girl's parents always assured him that it could not possibly have happened.) It is more like saying: "You made a mistake about the relationship between you as a subject and your signifiers"; that is, we are completely outside "reality". To say "this thought is mine, not yours", or vice versa, is not a fact of reality. What must have troubled Lacan was, in short, the problematic relationship between the subject (Lacan himself) and what he says and writes (Lacan's seminars and writings). In other words, Lacan posed the same problem that psychotic subjects pose when they say, for example, "My thoughts are not mine, they are thought by the Other". Where to place the mark of subjectivity? When certain Lacanians mechanically repeat the formulas and statements of Lacan, or of those who instructed them, *who* is doing the thinking?

Subjects very often believe that they are thinking simply because they are convinced that the words they use are doing the thinking for them. If I repeat something that I basically do not understand, such as "The psyche is extended, and knows nothing about it",[1] I am convincing myself that my thinking lies in the sentence itself. To believe we understand is to think that what we say thinks for us.

With regard to Brain, on the surface Lacan is saying "Brain says to Kris 'it may be true that I don't *actually* plagiarize, but my devouring desire for the ideas of others remains'"; anyway, his insistence on this point tells us something else. In my opinion, Lacan is actually saying "there is *nothing* of my thought that I can transmit". Because, as we have seen, to transmit is to simplify and to trivialize, while Lacan wants to tell us . . . *what* he *is*.

But how can we teach what we are? Each one of us is a pure unrepeatable event, and it is against this background of unrepeatability that the endless web of meaning unravels: writings, speeches, quotations, summaries, teaching. . . . But for Lacan, meaning – transmission – misses the subject as event, the solipsistic background of all communication and ultimately of all realism.[2] It's as if Lacan were saying to his listeners and pupils: "Eat my brain!" It is the allegorical, cannibalistic and savage form of teaching: eating, if not the body, certainly the brain of the Master. "Eat me!" Lacan seems to say.

In *The Lesson*, Ionesco (1951) left us an extraordinary parable: a pedagogical relationship is one which ends with the elimination of the pupil. My pupils must cease to be themselves and become me, the master! But here Lacan seems to be showing us the opposite path: to be a pupil, you must devour the master. Yet to devour the other in order to be the other is an illusion. The other's brain is not the other's being.

Paradoxically, in founding a school, Lacan desperately affirmed the impossibility of teaching. Hence the enigmatic character of his writing, which constantly repeats to us: *You will never be able to think what I think*! But he needed an audience to devour what he thought. In fact, when for years I attended Lacan's seminars, I would literally devour everything he said. But devouring is still not understanding. What is understanding?

Lacan identifies with Brain insofar as Brain seems to be saying: "I will never be able to write myself. Anything I write that makes sense will always come from the Other".

This is what happens in certain forms of schizophrenia, in thought control syndrome, for example. Schizophrenic subjects say: "It's not me speaking or thinking: the Other is speaking and thinking through me". They say so because at heart it's true. Is to speak, to think, really to state ourselves? Schizophrenics need to say something unspeakable and unthinkable, and everything else is . . . a suggestion, copying.

Do I want to say that Lacan was psychotic? In a way he once said it himself: "I am psychotic for the simple reason that I have always tried to be rigorous" (Lacan, 1976, p. 9). Psychosis is an attempt (*essai*) of rigour. And it is quite significant that he began his career addressing psychotic writing, including his patient Aimée's poems (Lacan, 1975 [1933]), and ended it discussing the writing of James Joyce (*Se23*), in whom he saw a psychotic structure. But these cases do not concern psychosis in the clinical sense. They regard the psychotic effects of wanting to cross a certain line, which, in the case of writing, is wanting to say something absolutely *singular*. Now, language is designed to state the generic, not the singular. The terms "table" and "stars" indicate all tables and all stars, not a single table or star in particular. We can of course give any name to a table and a star, but a name is the tag put on something that cannot state its singularity. We can only try to circumscribe the singularity from general terms. And this applies all the more to subjective singularity.

Notes

1 This is a famous and very enigmatic statement by Freud (1941).
2 The idea that solipsism and strict realism are equivalent was advocated by Wittgenstein (1922) in the *Tractatus* (5.64).

Chapter 14

The Party and the Pope . . .

To come back to Lacan's texts.

Lacan's controversy with Kris betrays an acrimony that is almost embarrassing for the reader and that certainly undermines the persuasiveness of his arguments.

For example, when Lacan refers to the discovery that Prof. Brain's colleague is in fact the plagiarist, he adds ironically that "it was Kris's big heart that opened its doors". He meant that Kris exculpated his patient: the latter is not the villain; if there's a scoundrel, it's the other man. Now, he adds, if I (Lacan) told him that, Kris would disagree: "He would tell me, with the seriousness proverbially attributed to the Pope, that he followed the grand principle of approaching problems from the surface" (*Écrits*, p. 329). What does the pope have to do with a Jew such as Kris? Is he saying that Kris is *pontificating*? The tone of Kris's essay is in actual fact more that of diplomatic propaganda. And why should Kris pontificate if Lacan were to tell him that out of the goodness of his big heart he exculpated the patient? The reader becomes suspicious of a controversy that seems somewhat over the top.

An answer may come from a recollection that Lacan himself gives, on another occasion, of a personal encounter, perhaps his only one, with Ernst Kris.

> I remember him at the Marienbad Congress [of 1936] where, the day after my address on the mirror stage, I took my leave, anxious as I was to get a feeling for the spirit of the time – a time full of promises – at the Olympics in Berlin. He kindly objected, "Ça ne se fait pas!" ("That isn't done!"), having already acquired that penchant for the respectable that perhaps influenced his approach here [in *Ego Psychology and Interpretation in Psychoanalytic Theory*].
>
> (*Écrits*, p. 501)

It's not clear whether Kris's reprimand was made in public or in private – if it had been done in public, even if "kindly", it would have had the sense of a public humiliation. But we don't know why Kris made that remark. Whether it was just because Lacan planned to leave before the end of proceedings or whether it was also because he intended to go to the Berlin Olympics, which – we should remember – were a propagandistic podium for Hitler's national-socialism (and at the time, most analysts were Jewish). In any case, the utterance was probably enough to

DOI: 10.4324/9781003388098-14

make Lacan harbour a certain resentment towards Kris. Note that they were almost the same age, Kris was just one year older than Lacan, and Lacan was 35 at the time: a certain paternalism from his peer must have seemed "pontifical" to him.

But who was Kris?

He was a man Lacan ought to have very much appreciated, being as he was an art expert. Kris was not only an analyst but also an important art historian, a pupil of the great Julius von Schlosser (the main inspirer of the Viennese school of art history); it seems that Schlosser said about Kris "he is my most original pupil". Kris, a member of Freud's inner circle, studied philosophy (Lacan had also taken several courses in philosophy) and became curator of the department of sculpture and applied arts at the Kunsthistorisches Museum in Vienna. In New York, beyond his activity as an analyst, Kris worked as a curator at the Metropolitan Museum. He was the foremost specialist in engraved jewellery and carvings of the Renaissance. Another art historian destined for great fame, the Viennese Ernst Gombrich, was his friend and pupil, and together they had planned to publish a volume on caricature.[1]

Kris was a typical product of the Austrian Jewish intelligentsia. Unlike the other two reprobates (according to Lacan) of ego psychology – Rudolph Löwenstein and Heinz Hartmann – Kris was certainly the analyst from the New York diaspora most akin to Lacan in terms of cultural versatility and intellectual openness. And Lacan himself admitted that, of the three, Kris was "the thinking head". As we shall see, this imaginary fraternity between Kris and Lacan is perhaps a key to understanding this part of Lacan's text and even his campaign against ego psychology in general.

It is also worth noting that Kris had emigrated to America in 1940, so by the time he published that text in 1948, he had been living in New York for eight years. Long enough to familiarize himself with the place, but not long enough to cease being what he in fact was: a Mitteleuropean analyst and intellectual. Someone Lacan would probably have liked to be: someone who was close to Freud in person and built a psychoanalytical school in one of the world's major cities.

It would be easy to say that Lacan (fore)sees a pontificating attitude in Kris because, in fact, he himself – as the years went by – took on more and more the attitude of the sententious Sibyl. The point is that, at the very time Lacan was dealing with Professor Brain, he was also trying to engage with the real pope.

In 1953, shortly before drafting and reading his "Rome Discourse" – which first launched his original ideas on the primacy of language and speech – he'd contacted his brother Marc-François, a Benedictine, to convince him that his theory was entirely consistent with the Christian message. He also asked his brother to arrange an audience with the pope – Pius XII at the time – to discuss the future of psychoanalysis in the Church with him. The audience was not granted, but this did not prevent him from going to a public audience with the pope at Castel Gandolfo in October 1953.[2] Not that he'd abjured his atheism – indeed, at the same time he also tried to contact the French Communist Party to propose his Discourse, which he considered a kind of cultural revolution. One may say that these were tactical manoeuvres in a frankly megalomaniac phase. I find it most meaningful that he was trying to have his contribution accepted at the same time by two radically antagonistic institutions such as the Communist Party and the papacy but which at the time clearly had one major feature in common: both were, in the West, the quintessence of totalitarian culture, because the Catholic Church wasn't yet the one that emerged after the Second Vatican Council: it was extremely conservative and anti-psychoanalytic. The position of the Church on such psychological matters was then mainly influenced by the Italian Franciscan friar Agostino Gemelli, a fascist psychologist and anti-Semite, hostile to psychoanalysis. And the Communist Party was different from what it would gradually become after the 20th Congress of the CPSU in 1956: it was Stalinist to the core, centralized and fanatical. And the PCF was, no less than the papacy, anti-Freudian. This fascination of Lacan's at the time for the two totalitarianisms hostile to psychoanalysis, however contradictory, should give us food for thought.

Claiming that poor Kris has a "Papal seriousness" has all the hallmarks of a projection. Lacan is actually mocking him when he writes: "An era of new comprehension begins" (*Écrits*, p. 329). But this was exactly what he thought about his own system of thought (which in the period 1953–54 was being presented publicly): that it announced an era of new comprehension. Lacan really does seem to be looking at himself in Kris's mirror.

In November 1955 Lacan held a conference in Vienna, "The Freudian Thing", in which, among other things, he criticized Anna Freud's use of the concept of the Ego in the second topography, on the grounds that she had somehow "thingified" it. The ego had been promoted by Sigmund Freud 35 years earlier (in *The Ego and the Id*), and here Lacan uses a metaphor based on the couple:

> From thirty-five years of cohabitation with the ego [*le moi*] under the roof of the second Freudian topography –including ten years of a rather stormy relationship, finally legitimized by the ministry of Miss Anna Freud in a marriage whose social credit has done nothing but grow ever since, so much so that people assure me it will soon request the Church's blessing – in short, from the most sustained work of psychoanalysts, you will draw nothing more than this drawer.
> (*Écrits*, p. 350)

What does Anna Freud – whose celibacy Lacan sardonically points out – a Jew and an atheist, have to do with the Church's blessing of a marriage (between the Ego and the second topography)? Wasn't ego psychology essentially composed of Jews? The point is that a short while back, it had been Lacan who'd sought a blessing from the pope. We see here at work, once again, a projection effect.

Notes

1 On Kris, Gombrich and caricature, see: Rose, 2007, Krüger, 2011. Krüger (2012) analyzes the account of the case of the Brain Eater by Kris as an example of Kris's theory of the grotesque.
2 See Roudinesco, 1992, pp. 274–275.

Chapter 15

Anti-Americanism

As for Lacan's anti-Americanism – which he would soften immensely over the years, almost converting it into outright admiration for the Americans, who were increasingly interested in his thought – it echoed an attitude that was quite typical of European intellectuals at the time and which still lingers on in certain circles, even though the United States now enjoy a pervasive cultural prestige. Lacan was Anglophile and anti-American, just like Freud. In fact, Lacan could have said, like Freud to Jones: "America is gigantic, but a gigantic mistake" (in Bettelheim, 2001). Freud didn't imagine that the United States would become, for decades, the country with the most psychoanalysts in the world, and Lacan didn't know that, after his death, his thought would have considerable success in America in certain intellectual areas (comparative literature, gender studies, history, cultural studies . . .), whereas Lacanianism would always remain completely marginal in, for example, Germany.

Though he had no direct experience of America, Lacan evidently made himself the spokesman for what was a widespread cliché at the time: that for *all* Americans what counts is social success, free enterprise, the market, business (but perhaps he was not aware that already at the time America had a far greater passion for religious matters than Europe).[1] And here Lacan inserts this theme – which then, as now, would have easily drawn applause from a French audience not immune to chauvinism – twisting, once again, Kris's text.

This extensive anti-Americanism has led to a major distortion, widespread even among analysts who have little to do with Lacanianism, of the history of psychoanalysis, in Latin countries in particular (Latin American countries included): the basic idea that American psychoanalysis, which developed in the 1950s, "betrayed" the original Mitteleuropean *Stimmung* of analysis. The rise of ego psychology, and then of other currents not born but established in America, is depicted as a Yankee colonization of old Europe. But quite the opposite is true: American psychoanalysis is the effect of an authentic colonization of the New World by mainly German-speaking and mainly Jewish expatriates. The United States had its specific psychiatric tradition, one that never welcomed psychoanalysis and which made a major comeback in the 1980s, trying to completely demolish the psychoanalytic edifice (in particular with the DSMs, the *Diagnostical and Statistical Manuals*

DOI: 10.4324/9781003388098-15

of Mental Disorders, the Bibles of contemporary psychiatry). Psychoanalysis in America was a transplant that boomed for decades, but it always remained a transplant and was therefore prone to rejection.

From the early post-war period Freud treated and trained mainly American patients, who at that time were the only ones who could afford to pay high fees. Yet American psychiatry, at the time, had strong reservations about psychoanalysis and viewed it as an unscientific and unproven theory. In this regard, it is interesting to consider what the American psychiatrist Joseph Wortis thought of his analysis with Freud and of Freud himself. Wortis (1994) already lists, in the 1930s, all the objections that will become canonical in the attacks against Freud in America from 1980 onwards.

Most of the major "American" psychoanalysts were born elsewhere and came to America quite late in life. Kris was born in Vienna and arrived in America at the age of 40. Heinz Hartmann, also born in Vienna, arrived at the age of 47. Rudolph Löwenstein, Lacan's analyst, born in Lodz, Poland, arrived at the age of 44. And we could continue the list with most of the famous "American" analysts.[2] Almost all of them came to the United States not because of any special fascination with America but simply because they were mostly Jews fleeing Nazi persecution and war. In other words, it is misleading to speak of "American psychoanalysis" and its misdeeds. We should instead speak of Austro-German-American psychoanalysis. Indeed, psychoanalysis, with its rebirth in the German-speaking world after the war, has always pursued close relations with the American schools, in a sort of continuity that can also be considered biographical, remaining immune to Kleinian influence.

It must also be said that ego psychology was often harshly criticized in the United States, mostly by other Austrian-German emigrants. The most famous is Herbert Marcuse (1955), heir of the Frankfurt School. Born in Berlin, he had emigrated to the United States at the age of 36, in 1934, also to escape Nazism. We can therefore view the great appeals for or against ego psychology, which became the dominant trend in the United States after the Second World War, as a debate that largely took place *within* the Austro-German intelligentsia that had emigrated to the United States.

As for me, since I think I'm fairly well acquainted with the United States, I'm also quite allergic to anti-Yankee or anti-Gringo catchphrases. I'm well aware that the United States is a large, complex, multifaceted country, where you can come across the best and the worst of everything, so trying to schematically label "the American mentality" always boils down to a xenophobic simplification.

But where does this urge, which is not only Lacanian, to label the analytical currents that flourished in the United States "tacky" come from? I would say it derives from something of a hereditary conflict. Insofar as the Europeans, including Lacan, claimed to be the legitimate heirs and perpetuators of Freud's work, it was necessary to portray the figureheads of the American schools as "completely Americanized", in other words as renegade analysts. It was necessary or very desirable to break the thread that united these analysts – starting with Anna Freud, who lived in London – to the original Austrian-German cradle. According to this propaganda, abandoning Europe was abandoning *real* psychoanalysis.

Notes

1 This anti-American cliché, widespread in French culture and especially among Lacanians, has been refuted with good arguments by Darian Leader (2021).
2 David Rapaport, of Hungarian origins, came to the United States at the age of 27. Erich Fromm, born in Frankfurt am Main, at the age of 34. And Heinz Kohut, born in Vienna, at the age of 27. Margareth Mahler, Hungarian, emigrated at the age of 41. Erik Erikson, also born in Frankfurt am Main, at the age of 31. Helen Deutsch, born in the Austrian part of polish Galicia, at the age of 51. Theodor Reik, who pioneered lay analysis in the United States, was born in Vienna and went to the United States at the age of 45. Edward Bibring, born in Galicia, at the age of 1941. Karen Horney, born near Hamburg, at the age of 47. More recently, Otto Kernberg, who was born in Vienna and had previously emigrated to Chile, moved to the United States at the age of 33.

Chapter 16

Eating Nothingness

When Lacan returns to the case of Professor Brain in 1958, in "The Direction of the Cure", his focus is no longer on acting out but rather on the diagnosis to be made on Brain. In the meantime, Kris had died (in February 1957).

Here, Lacan is again unfaithful to Kris's text and states that Kris is trying to prove to the patient that he wants to be a plagiarist in order to prevent himself from actually being one. But this is not what Kris says. Even Fink (2004, p. 57) admits that this is a "very creative" interpretation by Lacan. Instead Lacan agrees with the first analyst that the patient was dominated by an "oral aggression", one that had, however, been inhibited. According to Lacan, his underlying drive was to devour and destroy the ideas of others, and as a defence against this impulse Brain feared he could end up copying and hence gave up publishing. Here too, the question that begs an answer is: why does he misunderstand Kris? To caricature his theses, to exclude from Kris's discourse any reference to the id, to bodily drives, to orality. This caricaturization of Kris's thesis makes it easier for Lacan to criticize and demolish him.

Again, according to Lacan, Kris thought that the fear of plagiarizing was a form of defence, whereas the real drive is that of being attracted to the ideas of others. This is a misinterpretation in Lacan's view, insofar as "it presupposes that defence and drive are concentric, the one being moulded, as it were, on the other" (*Écrits*, p. 501). Which is to say that the drives are a more interior circle, defences a more exterior one, in the same way as the walls of a citadel are more external in respect to the palace. According to Lacan, Kris believes that the confession of a passion for fresh brains is a confirmation of his own interpretation, while Lacan thinks that it is the confession of an acting out, and for Lacan an acting out is a correction of the analyst's intervention by the patient. It amounts to the latter saying "you've missed the point!" ("*vous êtes à côté*"). But this interpretation of Lacan's is in fact based on two important distortions of what Kris wrote.

On the one hand, as we saw, Brain had been looking for that menu for some time, well before Kris's interpretation; we cannot therefore say that it was an acting out challenging the interpretation. Unless we imagine that here Lacan considers this fact that the patient *says* to the analyst that he's looking for fresh brains, an acting rather than the *act* of looking for them. But according to Freud the passage of an

DOI: 10.4324/9781003388098-16

act into speech is quite the opposite of an acting. The second distortion is to ascribe to Kris an interpretation that is not in fact his, as we've just seen. Kris, being a true Freudian, does not lose sight of the inaugural, I would call it, destructive oral drive.

It is at this point that Lacan changes his register of discourse: while before he referred to Kris in the third person, he starts addressing him with *vous* (not *tu*). He turns him into his interlocutor, now that he is dead and cannot answer. He suddenly starts talking to his antagonist. But he is talking to a spectre. Indeed, a spectre is haunting the West: The spectre of the (imaginary) Freudian heritage, which reminds me the Maltese Falcon in the film of this title: that this golden heritage is made with the stuff of dreams.

And it is at this point that he evokes the Marienbad "incident", if we want to call it that, when Kris rebuked him with "*Ça ne se fait pas!*" In short, in the text his relationship with Kris suddenly becomes personalized, dramatized, and simultaneously the text becomes more and more enigmatic, as he says himself: "Was this what lead you astray, Ernst Kris? . . . [but] the times themselves are out of joint [*en chicane*]". *Chicaner* means to quibble but also to take a circuitous route or to zigzag, like in a slalom. And indeed, from this point on the style of his writing becomes *en chicane*. The great *chicane* is the following: according to Lacan it's not that Prof. Brain does not steal; the point is that "he steals *nothing*" ["c'est qu'il vole *rien*"]. This is what, according to Lacan, Kris doesn't grasp, lost as he is in his analysis of defences.

Often Lacan points out that the French term *rien*, nothing, comes from the Latin *rem*, accusative of *res*, thing. It's as if in French when one says "*Je ne mange rien*", one says "I do not eat a thing".

This is one of those cases Freud (1910) would have put on the tally of antithetical meanings of primal words – but no word, present-day linguistics says, is primal; everything in a language is secondary. After all, this is true in English too: when one says "*I don't say anything*", with *anything* having the antithetical sense of *nothing*. So, for present quantum physics, "void" and "full" are the same thing.

I would say that this is an ironic *chicane* intrinsic to the history of every language, whereby the accusative of *res*, thing, in another language becomes *nonthing*, *nothing*. There are plenty of examples of etymological irony in languages, with something often ending up denoting its opposite.

> Contrary to what you believe [Kris], it is not his defence against the idea of stealing that makes him believe he steals. It is that it never occurs to him [*ne lui vient pas à l'idée*], or just barely crosses his mind, that he could have an idea of his own.
>
> (*Écrits*, p. 502)

Or, put in a less zigzagging way: it's not as if the patient defends himself from a temptation by thinking he's already succumbed to it; it's that he cannot conceive of an idea as being his own, not unlike the case I mentioned of the analysand who could only give an interpretation if it wasn't her own but originating from the Other (the analyst).

The following year Lacan would give a seminar, "The Ethics of Psychoanalysis (Sem 7)", entirely focused on the notion of *chose*, thing, derived from Freud's *das Ding*. I cannot dwell too long here on this absolutely peculiar seminar. I shall only point out that this is the only seminar in which he develops the concept of "thing", a concept he would never take up again, at least not in the sense he gave it in this seminar, whereas it's a notion that was to enjoy huge success among authors inspired by Lacan. I have the impression, however, that Lacanians haven't enquired sufficiently into why he abandoned the concept after 1960. They usually say that the concept of "thing" – which is expressed when he tries to define what is ethical for psychoanalysis – was reabsorbed into the concept of object *a*, one he used even before that seminar. I shall leave the question open.

Now, to put it simply, for Lacan what we call ethical is our orbiting around a *Ding*, a thing, which usually takes the form of a void, an *athing*, we could call it. It's an emptiness we can never seize, never grasp once and for all, but which somehow guides us and which calls us to some sort of loyalty. Hence his charming analysis of Sophocles' *Antigone* – to the point that Lacan could have turned it into a complex in its own right, the Antigone complex. The complex that leads to heroic sacrifice *for nothing*. Antigone sacrifices herself by breaking the law of the city, which prohibits the burial of Polynices, her brother killed in battle against the city. Antigone performs the symbolic act of burying him. Now, for Lacan, Polynices's body is Antigone's "thing", a sort of *unicum* that asserts itself, but through his absence. Because, after all, Polynices is dead, he is a *rien*. So, saying that to be ethical is to remain true to one's Thing is the same as saying that to be ethical is to not give up on one's emptiness. The thing that's most precious to us is . . . nothing. A thing on the borders of being.

With regard to anorexia, Lacan would speak of object *rien*. Lacan had already added to his list of fundamental erogenous objects (breasts, faeces, penis) adding the phoneme, the gaze, the voice (corresponding objects of the scopic drive and the invocatory drive) and the object *rien*, nothing. The object *nothing* is another erotic, so to speak, object, but to which erogenous zone does it correspond? In the case of anorexia, to the oral zone, apparently. But in fact object-nothing has no specific erogenous zone: it seems to have its erogenous counterpart in every part of the body; it is the object of the erogenous body as such.

This is the Lacanian dialectic – exemplified by the fact that *res*, the thing, is a *rien* – that we must accept if we want to understand Lacan, even without becoming Lacanians of *l'école*. If you do not accept this dialectic, you will feel only contempt for Lacan. It amounts to accepting that in the human world, in other words, the negative is at work, that not everything is a relationship between positive objects. If you are a positivist, you will not accept a single line of what Lacan said and wrote. In short, we must think, with Hegel, that history, life, is also constituted by the negative, or lack, as Lacan says. We could say that the human world is not an analogical world, a mimetic world; it is a digital one consisting of bits: 0 works and it is essential, no less than 1. The fact that a current does not flow is just as important as the fact that a current does flow. Fullness reverses into emptiness, and vice versa. Along these lines, we can then say that Prof. Brain is a bulimic of nothingness. True, he does eat fresh brains, that is, *some thing*, but insofar as these brains are the signifier of ideas: he thinks he is eating a dish, but in fact he is eating a signifier, something that is not there. As he believes he has no "brain" (no ideas), he eats ideas from the outside, that is, no thing.

"Love is giving something you don't have to someone who doesn't want it".[1] A positively absurd statement. But for Lacan, love, like everything human, is *logical*: it is connected to the logos, to language, in which the negative works only too well! Anorexia, too, he stresses, is "mental" (in English *nervosa*), that is, logical. The anorexic acts by eating nothing.

Note

1 For example, in "Seminar 8" on transference.

Chapter 17

The Raft of Skinny Virgins

But what did Lacan think exactly about anorexia nervosa at the time?

In his 1957 seminar, "The Object Relation", he had said:

> Mental anorexia is not a *not eating*, but an *eating nothing*. I insist: this means *eating nothing*. Nothing is precisely something that exists on the symbolic plane. It is not a *nicht essen*, it is a *nichts essen*. This point is indispensable for the understanding of anorexia. What happens in specific is that the child eats nothing, which is something other than a negation of the activity.
>
> (*Se4, 184–5*[1])

In other words, anorexia is not the negation, the elimination of the oral drive, but its triumph. Except that for Lacan the drives are structured by the symbolic, so only by means of the symbolic can a nothing become an object, a something. Like the zero in mathematics or the empty set in set theory. The anorexic binges on nothing.[2]

We could also say that anorexia is akin to the fear of death. The ancient philosophers said we should not fear death, because death is nothing to those who are dead; "if I die, I am not there". But they missed the point. The anxiety of dying is not a fear of nothing, it is a fear of something very specific: of Nothingness. Nothingness threatens us, devastates us. And in fact no Epicurean reasoning has ever alleviated our fear of the nothingness that is death. In the case of the anorexic, however, nothingness is what gives her enjoyment.

And as the ancient Greeks knew, nothingness can also save our life, just as Ulysses, whose name was Nobody for the Cyclops, saved his own life.

Lacan's basic idea at the time seems to be the following: the anorexic starves herself – "eats nothingness" – to preserve her desire. In relation with a mother who stuffs her child to prove her love, the child saves itself as a subject, that is, as a desiring being, by eating nothing, thus signifying a demand for love. Lacan writes:

> But the child does not always fall asleep in this way in the bosom of being, especially if the Other, which has its own ideas about her needs, interferes and, instead of what she does not have, stuffs her with the smothering baby food it does have, that is, confuses the care it provides with the gift of its love.

DOI: 10.4324/9781003388098-17

> It is the child who is the most lovingly fed who refuses food and employs her refusal as if it were a desire (anorexia nervosa).
>
> (*Écrits*, p. 524)

Here too Lacan diverges from an idea that is widespread among analysts: that the mothers of future anorexics, of children who do not eat, don't really love their sons or daughters and conceal this lack of love by lavishing on them attentions that satisfy their needs but not their desires. Instead – Lacan seems to be saying – the Other (the mother) can sincerely love her creature; the point is that providing care doesn't amount to offering the gift of love. Here it is a matter of the mother's failure to signify, not of any deficiency in love on her part. And, as we mentioned, for Lacan love means giving what we do not have. By eating nothingness, that is, that which is missing, the anorexic reinstates a dissatisfaction without which there can be no desire. If desire is satisfied as a demand, it risks cancelling itself out as a desire: if I'm hungry and eat, I'll be full but I shall no longer wish to eat. Desire implies a constituent dissatisfaction. The rejection of food offered by the mother is the only means the subject finds to weaken maternal domination.

But what's the relation of the signifier "fresh brains" to ideas and the mind? At this point Lacan evokes the Russian linguist – and friend of his – Roman Jakobson (1971), who developed the concept of *metonymy*. For Jakobson, language has two axes, one paradigmatic, corresponding to metaphor ("one thing for another"), and another syntagmatic, corresponding to metonymy ("one thing after another"). Metaphor and metonymy are two rhetorical figures. A textbook example of metonymy: "the crown" to mean the king. The crown is only a part of the king, an appendage, but by naming this part I am signifying the whole. The crown is metonymically *close* to the king. Some metonyms are so common that they become catachresis, that is, proper nouns; for example, the English "the neck of the bottle". In short, Lacan seems to be saying that fresh brains (understood as a dish) are not a metaphor but a metonymy of the mind, insofar as brain and mind are contiguous entities (a brain has no resemblance to the mind).

Now, we can observe that from this point on, Lacan's text indulges, I would say, in an unrestrained metonymic shifting. After having presented us with the concept, he practices it to the limits of unreadability.

> You [Kris] treat the patient as if he were obsessed, but he throws you a line with his food fantasy, giving you the opportunity to be a quarter-of-an-hour ahead of the nosology of your time by providing a diagnosis of anorexia nervosa [*anorexie mentale*].
>
> (*Écrits*, p. 502)

Now, this diagnosis of Prof. Brain as an anorexic cannot but leave us baffled. How does this case relate to anorexics, usually adolescent girls who refuse to eat? But even anorexics, as we've seen, are "girls who eat nothing". In fact, most of them are manic, that is, energetic and buoyant, ego-syntonic, stuffed and bursting with nothingness.

Anorexia, in this case, concerns the mental realm, concerns the desire on which the idea lives, and this leads us to the scurvy that rages on the raft on which I embark him [Kris's patient] with the skinny virgins.

(*Écrits*, p. 502)

The metonymic slide here unsettles us, even if we cling to the raft of some signifiers to avoid drowning in the tide of his discourse. Calling anorexic women "skinny virgins" is also quite clever; it emphasizes that anorexics proper not only do not eat but are also *anerotic*, in the sense that they do not "consume" sexual relations with men, unless these relations are sublime, strictly *mental*. (Today, a distinction is made between hysterical anorexics, that is, neurotic anorexics, and mental anorexics in the strict sense of the term, which appear to be more on the side of psychosis. Lacan seems to refer to the latter.) They may have long and romantic relationships with a man, but they won't let themselves be touched by him.

But what's the place of the raft and the scurvy here? Lacan is most probably alluding to the *radeau* (raft) of the *Medusa*, a terrible incident dating back to 1816, but which everyone in France is familiar with thanks to a famous painting by Théodore Géricault, which can be admired at the Louvre. The *Méduse* was a French frigate that ran aground in the Atlantic. A large part of the crew abandoned the stranded ship in the shallows of the sea and drifted on a raft that they built. During the horrifying voyage, the lack of food and water led to cases of cannibalism and chaotic riots. In the end only a few castaways were saved. Scurvy was a disease common among sailors due to a lack of vitamin C intake. Here Lacan seems to be alluding to the episodes of cannibalism on the raft and, through scurvy, to the lack

Figure 17.1 The Raft of the *Medusa*

of food. He dazzlingly constructs a metonymy reminiscent of the style of Luis de Góngora; for this reason, Lacan's style is often branded as baroque Gongorism.

Professor Brain is a quasi-cannibal embarked on the raft of the *Medusa*, in a desperate drift in which he suffers from a lack not of vitamin C, but of "ideas of his own". The castaways ate human flesh; Brain eats nothingness, of which brains are a metonymy.

Here the Lacanian text takes on more and more the form of a raft adrift. On the basis of his fundamental principle: that discourse must have the same form as that which it discusses. One cannot speak of the irrational in an exceedingly rational manner; discourse must somehow have the form of what it speaks of.

And to conclude this section dedicated to Brain by Lacan, the last two enigmatic statements:

> To wipe desire off the map [*carte*] when it is already covered over in the patient's landscape is not the best way of following Freud's teaching.
>
> Nor is it a way of getting rid of depth, for it is on the surface that depth is seen, as when one's face breaks out in pimples on holidays.
>
> (*Écrits*, p. 503)

Carte means map and menu and an identity document. We can therefore read that Kris's purported map does not really reproduce the landscape, Brain as subject – it doesn't really describe his mind – because desire is absent from the map. In other words, what's absent from Kris's menu is desire – which, according to Lacan, is the essential paradigm of Freud's teaching. But this criticism is hard to uphold, because Kris sees a desire at the root of the symptom: the desire to eat and mangle the ideas of others, a devouring oral drive.

As for depth, Lacan too advocated an idea of the unconscious as something on the surface – for him psychoanalysis is not a depth psychology. But he doesn't believe that from a technical point of view "taking things from the surface" is the right way to "superficialise" the unconscious. Because depth, or rather desire, shines through under the scaly dermatitis, the scabies that blemish a face. A menu-map that does not designate desire is objectionable, and it is inedible.

And why does the under-skin manifest itself behind the scales specifically on feast days? Is it the metonymic feast of language through which Lacan invites us to the escape routes of signification?

Notes

1 Seminar of 27 February 1957.
2 For a Lacanian approach to anorexia, see Cosenza (2023).

Chapter 18

"Annie Reich's" Countertransference

Now, let us go back in time, to 1954, when Lacan held his seminar on "Freud's Writings on Technique". Here he confronts not only Kris but various other non-French analysts: Margaret Little, Anna Freud, Melanie Klein, Michael Balint. It will be useful to take a close look at how he structures this debate.

His first comment is on a 1951 article on counter-transference by a psychoanalyst. . . . Here Lacan is victim of another oversight: he believes he's quoting Annie Reich (1951), but in fact he was quoting Margaret Little,[1] a British psychoanalyst who had published her paper on the same topic (counter-transference) in the same issue of the same *International Journal* and whose essay followed Annie Reich's in this same issue. This is why I'll write "Annie Reich", despite the fact that the comments discussed are those of Margaret Little (1951).[2]

Lacan says:

For the authors in question, for Annie Reich, nothing else matters but the recognition by the subject, *hic et nunc*, of the intentions of his discourse. And his intentions only ever have value in their implications *hic et nunc*, in the immediate exchange. The subject may well describe himself taking on the grocer or the hairdresser – in fact, he is bawling out the person he's talking to, that is to say the analyst.

There is some truth in that. The slightest experience of conjugal life will tell you that there is always an implicit demand of some sort in the fact that one spouse relates to the other what got his goat during the day, rather than the other way round. But it may also stem from a concern to inform the other of some incident worth knowing about. Both are true. It is a question of knowing on which aspect one should throw some light.

As the following story told by Annie Reich shows, things do sometimes go even further. Certain of its features are a bit confused, but everything points to the fact that it is a training analysis, or in any case, the analysis of someone whose area of interest is very close to psychoanalysis.

The analysand had occasion to make a radio broadcast on a topic that intensely interested the analyst himself [I stress that Lacan here masculinizes Annie Reich, and we should ask ourselves why – *my note*] – these things happen.

DOI: 10.4324/9781003388098-18

It so happened that he gave this broadcast a few days after his mother's death. Now everything points to the fact that the mother in question plays an extremely important role in the patient's fixations. He is certainly very affected by this mourning, but he nonetheless fulfils his obligations in a particularly brilliant manner. The next session, he arrives in a state of stupor close to confusion. Not only is it impossible to get anything out of him, but what he does say is surprising in its lack of coordination. The analyst interprets boldly – *You are in this state because you think I greatly begrudge you your success on the radio the other day, with this topic which, as you know, personally interests me in the highest degree.* There we have it!

The rest of the account shows that it took a year for the subject to recover from this shock-interpretation, which hadn't failed to have some effect, since he had instantly recovered his spirits.

This shows you that the fact that the subject comes out of a confused state of mind following an intervention by the analyst by no means proves that it was effective in the strictly therapeutic, structuring sense of the word, namely that it was, in the analysis, true. On the contrary.

Annie Reich brought the subject back to a sense of the unity of his ego. Suddenly he tears himself out of the confusion in which he found himself, saying to himself – *Here is someone who points out to me that indeed everything is much of a muchness and that life goes on.* And he starts off, gets going again – the effect is instantaneous. It is impossible, in the analytic experience, to consider the subject's change of style as being the proof of the correctness of an interpretation. I consider the proof of the correctness of an interpretation to lie in the confirmatory material the subject supplies. And even that needs to be put more subtly.

After a year, the subject realizes that his state of confusion was linked to the backlash of his reactions to mourning, which he had only been able to overcome by inverting them. I refer you at this point to the psychology of mourning, whose depressive side some of you are sufficiently familiar with.

(*Sem 1*, 30)

At first blush one might think that "Reich's" intervention is wrong because it is a crude expression of the counter-transference of the analyst that she is talking about. The analyst is envious of his patient's success and attributes his state of debilitation to a response, we do not know to what extent conscious, to this envy of the analyst's. Lacan, however, criticizes this intervention not insofar as it could be false; on the contrary: "Not only can we concede that the subject had been prey to the feelings that the analyst imputed to him, it is even extremely probable" (*Sem 1*, 32). "Extremely probable": almost certain. But for a very simple reason, he adds: generally speaking, *sentiments are always reciprocal*. A provocative statement. What about unrequited loves and likings? Lacan means to say that unless a third term is brought in to de-reciprocate, feelings tend to be reciprocal. If someone looks at me with dislike, I will also feel dislike towards them. If someone else smiles sincerely at me, I shall tend to smile back. If this symmetry does not occur, it is because there is something more that breaks the reciprocity. If someone smiles at me, I may not reciprocate the smile for different reasons: if I consider this person a rogue, for example, or a fool. An extra-relational evaluation, so to speak, can suspend reciprocity.

Now, the fact that the analyst envies the patient (Lacan calls this envy "jeal-ousy" in the original) and therefore harbours a feeling of irritation towards him is already enough to vex him. The irritation is present virtually at least. Therefore, if the analyst says this to him – "You are hostile because you think I'm irritated with you" – this sparks off the very existence of this reciprocity. "Reich's" commentary is therefore to be criticized not because the analyst is saying something false but because it is "something prior to truth and falsity" (*Sem 1*, 33).

And Lacan adds:

The analyst here believes herself authorised [*autorisé – sic*[3]] to offer what I will call an interpretation from *ego to ego*, or from equal to equal [*d'égal à égal*] . . . in other words, an interpretation whose foundation and mechanism cannot in any way be distinguished from that [*sic*] of projection.

(*Sem 1*, 32)

And he specifies: I am not saying erroneous projection, because projection cre-ates ipso facto a symmetrical retro-projection (let's say that projective statements verify themselves) but because we remain at the level of the ego or of the self, that is to say of what – according to Lacan – is imaginary reciprocity, as in a mirror. Therefore, "In the interpretation of defences, there should always be at least a third term".

Such a comment on this counter-transferential intervention sounds even more important today, ever since the practice of exploiting interpretation "from ego to ego, from *égal à égal*" – as Lacan says – has become generalized. Today it is known as self-disclosure: this is when analysts tell patients facts and anecdotes about themselves. Little does not seem to have been influenced by Sandor Ferenczi (1928), who was the first to theorize this opening of the analyst to his patients.[4] Self-disclosure developed into so-called "relationalism", the idea that everything is played out in the relationship "between two persons", analyst and patient. (The success in Italy of the expression "the analyst reacts person-to-person" – rather than "subject-to-subject" or "mind-to-mind" – is probably a sign of the influence of Catholic philosophical personalism.) It goes counter to the approach of the later Freud (1937), who essentially identified analysis with a work of historical con-struction or reconstruction (*Konstruktion*) of the subject's life. Here, the focus is instead on the *hic et nunc*, on the present face-to-face between the two subjects, with little relevance given to the reconstruction of past processes. W.R. Bion went so far as to say that we should consider the patient who comes into the session, even if we've been seeing him for years, completely new, unknown. For this rea-son, Bion recommends that analysts suspend "memory and desire". They shouldn't remember anything they did with the patient in the past, as all that counts is their interaction with him *here and now*, and they shouldn't even have any desire to analyse (nor should they be distracted by their personal desires). Analysts must act as pure reactive emotional mirrors, which is precisely what Little did. But the question arises: is an analyst trained as an analyst because he *desired* to be one? And if he desired to be one, what does he think is desirable in an analyst?

In fact, already at the time of Little's article, it had become common practice to give more and more prominence to analysts' "lived experiences", essentially to their counter-transferences. For example, it's become a ritual in supervisions today to ask the analyst who presents a case "And what did *you* feel?" The emotional reactions of the analyst are undoubtedly important and significant, but the present tendency is to make them the very centre of the analytic relationship. In some cases, the analyst, when writing about a case, relates his or her own childhood memories, dreams and experiences evoked by the patient's memories, dreams and lived experiences. The idea is that the "hierarchy" inherent to the analytical relationship can be overcome through this ever-thicker plot between the phantasmatic life of the patient and that of the analyst. It's an "equal to equal", symmetric relationship, resembling that between friends or spouses. It's equivalent to not wearing a lab coat with patients in psychiatry. It's the triumph of analytical democracy. . . . We can say that, within this perspective, analysts offer themselves as "good friends" or "good spouses". There's no incommensurability or asymmetry between the analyst's position and that of the analysand.

Lacan would of course be very harsh on today's mainstream psychoanalysis, which tends to interpret everything in terms of transference and counter-transference.

If today the analysand says in a session that they've encountered someone who irritated them, the analyst will say "you're irritated with me". But for Lacan this isn't entirely false. A friend of mine who was a "ladies' man", who knew the spiritual intimacies of women quite well, used to say to me that when a woman you're pursuing complains to you about her life, then it's a sign that she doesn't want to come to bed with you. A woman who reciprocates your desire will tend to give you a satisfied image of herself. This is generally true: complaining about one's woes excessively is an aggressive act (as Lacan pointed out here); it is a vindictive and violent request for help. It is like saying to the other "You're of no use to me! What are you doing there?" Angrily attacking a third party when you are talking to someone is a way of attacking this someone you're talking to. But to think that in a session this is always the case is indeed a mistake; it's the night in which all cows are black. An analysand has his or her *own* problems beyond their relationship with you as an analyst, and sharing them with you is a part of transference.

This leads many Lacanians today to the opposite excess: to avoid any interpretation of transference. Their motto is "not interpretation *of* transference, interpretation *in* transference". This also seems to me one sided. In my opinion, a dream that is clearly a transference dream should be interpreted as such. What is overlooked about countertransference is that it cannot be reduced to the conscious feelings of the analyst – like "he irritates me!", "she is fascinating!", "he bores me to death!" – because it is indeed unconscious. As transference often is. Countertransference manifests itself obliquely; it cannot be identified with the affective consciousness of the analyst. It may reveal itself through a slip of the analyst, for example.

Countertransference is expressed by symptoms, missed acts and dreams (this is why we speak of countertransferential dreams), not just by explicit feelings. And countertransference is not simply a reaction to the transference of the analysand; for this reason I would not speak of countertransference but, as Elvio Fachinelli has proposed, of transference of the analyst. It often establishes itself even before the transference of the analysand. In any case, Lacan's criticism of what he called the "English school"[5] is clear: the analyst is not "a person like the patient" but a figure who is not in fact symmetrical to the patient. According to Lacan, the analyst is above all an interpreter, while the person actually analysing is the patient – who is called, for this reason, the analysand.

Notes

1 Margareth Little (1901–1994), British analyst, was analysed by Ella Freeman Sharpe and by D.W. Winnicott. She is well known because of her approach to the analyst's counter-transference, and her article quoted by Lacan is considered seminal on the topic of counter-transference.
2 The interesting thing is that Lacan somehow "knew" that it was Margaret Little, since he places her in the "English school", which is true. Years later, in his seminar on *Angoisse* (*Sem* 10, 135), Lacan will quote another text by Little (1957) and will refer to the essay by Little again, this time calling her by her real name but also committing another lapsus: he says that he had commented on her in his second seminar, while he had in fact mentioned her in the first one, calling her Annie Reich.
3 Of course, this is a mistake of the editor of this seminar.
4 See also Rachman, 1998.
5 Perhaps Lacan did not know that Annie Reich lived in America. But in fact, he was thinking of the real author of the paper, Margaret Little, who was indeed British. He was *talking about* "Annie Reich", but in fact he was *thinking about* Margaret Little.

Chapter 19

Anna Freud's Counter-Defence

In the seminar of 17 February 1954, Lacan engages in a comparison between Anna Freud and Melanie Klein, which seems to go in Klein's favour. But I say *seems*, because things are actually more complex.

I quote the passage from Anna Freud's article that Lacan quotes in full in his seminar.[1] It concerns a young patient who entered analysis because of a severe anxious state that was disrupting her life and her studies.

> Her attitude toward me was friendly and frank, but I noticed that in all her communications she carefully avoided making any allusion to her symptom. She never mentioned anxiety attacks which took place between the analytic sessions. If I myself insisted on bringing her symptom into the analysis or gave interpretations of her anxiety which were based on unmistakable indications in her associations, her friendly attitude changed. On every such occasion the result was a volley of contemptuous and mocking remarks. *The attempt to find a connection between the patient's attitude and her relation to her mother was completely unsuccessful* [This sentence is italicized in the original but not in Lacan's transcription. *Benvenuto's note*]. Both in consciousness and in the unconscious that relation was entirely different. In these repeated outbursts of contempt and ridicule the analyst found herself at a loss and the patient was, for the time being, inaccessible to further analysis. As the analysis went deeper, however, we found that these affects did not represent a transference reaction in the true sense of the term and were not connected with the analytic situation at all. They indicated the patient's customary attitude toward herself whenever emotions of tenderness, longing, or anxiety were about to emerge in her affective life. The more powerfully the affect forced itself upon her, the more vehemently and scathingly did she ridicule herself. The analyst became the recipient of these defensive reactions only secondarily, because she was encouraging the demands of the patient's anxiety to be worked over in consciousness. The interpretation of the content of the anxiety, even when this could be correctly inferred from other communications, could have no result so long as every approach to the affect only intensified her defensive reaction. It was impossible to make that content conscious until we had brought into consciousness and so rendered inoperative

DOI: 10.4324/9781003388098-19

the patient's method of defending herself against her affects by contemptuous disparagement – a process which had become automatic in every department of her life. Historically this mode of defence by means of ridicule and scorn was explained by her identification of herself with her dead father, who used to try to train the little girl in self-control by making mocking remarks when she gave way to some emotional outburst. The method had become stereotyped through her memory of her father, whom she had loved dearly. The technique necessary in order to understand this case was to begin with the analysis of the patient's defence against her affects and to go on to the elucidation of her resistance in the transference. Then, and then only, was it possible to proceed to the analysis of her anxiety itself and of its antecedents.

(Sel, 77–8)

Lacan's comments go somewhat in the same direction as his criticism of "Annie Reich": according to him, Anna Freud took the patient's symptom in analysis – the ridiculing of what the analyst said – as a transferential issue, even though here Anna Freud then traces the behaviour with the analyst back to the patient's relationship with her father. This allows Lacan to criticize a tendency – which would later expand almost to occupy the entire field – to lead practically everything back to the mother–child relationship. The analyst, even if male, is seen as a substitute for the mother, and therefore everything leads back to the primary, precocious relations between nurturer and child. This tendency, strongly reinforced by John Bowlby's successful attachment theory, currently dominates psychological, but often even psychoanalytic, approaches to subjectivity: the mother is considered the cause of everything that matters in the life of a subject, so much so that I almost feel like emulating Melitta Schmideberg, who in ranting against her mother in public would shout: "Whatever happened to the father?"[2] (And one cannot help but think that this shouting at such an overwhelmingly imposing mother was a dramatic, very personal reproach to Melanie for having eclipsed the shady, low-profile father, rather than the strong father Melitta would have needed to slip away from maternal engulfment.) The function, not to say of the father but of a third person in relation to the mother/child pair, is mostly ignored today. At the time Lacan already perceived this tendency.

Against the inclination to dualize the relationship between mother and child, Lacan invokes the Oedipus complex, stressing the *complex*, that is, complexity. Even though the standard Oedipus theorized by Freud does seem rather simple, it opens up to complexity, which is established whenever a dual relationship – which, as we saw, is a relationship of specular reciprocity in Lacan's view – is interrupted and fractured by the intrusion of a "third" element. When the analyst interprets her relationship with the patient as a replica of another dual relationship, the mother/ daughter relationship, she goes off track. In fact, Anna Freud realizes that what is in play is an identification of the patient with the father, who in addition has the characteristic of being dead: not present. In a certain sense, for Lacan, the third element, whether the father or anyone else, is always "dead"; it eludes the reciprocity of presence, it eludes the complete pairing of the I/you relationship, it introduces an absence, which he considers essential.

Lacan's insistence on the triangularity of the Oedipus as complexity is probably inspired by the classical three-body problem in physics and mathematics. As we know, when considering the gravitational interactions of three bodies – earth, moon and sun – there is no single solution, but several equilibria are possible. This is an element of indeterminism within a vision, like gravitation, that appears deterministic. The Oedipus is like the three-body problem: the third body, the father, introduces an element of indeterminism that breaks the linear interdependence between mother and son. Oedipus means that human beings are not predictable.

Focusing entirely on the mother/child relationship reflects a positivist mentality: it is a *fact* that a child reacts to a mother before anyone else, that there are two presences. The introduction of the father, of a third, means the introduction of an absence, or of a lesser presence, and this is very difficult to accept for a way of thinking that excludes the negative in the things. For a positivist it is easy to understand why a mother sacrifices herself for her child, much more difficult to understand why some people sacrifice themselves for Freedom, for Socialism, for the Fatherland . . . for things that are not present.

Lacan writes:

> What Anna Freud calls the analysis of the defences against affect is only one step in her own understanding and not in that of the subject. Once she realises that she is on the wrong track in believing that the subject's defence is a defence against herself, she can then analyse the resistance to the transference.
>
> (*Se1*, 80. *Sem1*, 82)

What does this mean? Probably that Anna Freud interprets the attitude of ridiculing what I would call a stormy heart as a defence against affection, because initially she had, wrongly, considered this attitude a defence in transference. She projects into the past a process that had taken place in the present. He adds, however, that Anna Freud eventually realizes that there is an absent third party at work: the father.

But Lacan tells us more: that the patient does not defend herself against *this* analyst; she resists (the shift from "defence" to "resistance" is relevant) the transference in itself.

Now, what Lacan finds unconvincing is designating as a defence what is a structuring of the ego: that is, the patient's profound identification with her father. When the father taunted her because she showed her feelings, he was not defending her against affections: he was inculcating a model into her, that of a certain stoic indifference. Anna Freud calls "defence against affects" a way of being of the subject that comes directly from the father (from the Other). For Lacan, the defence – not allowing oneself to be overwhelmed by affects, in this case by anxiety – is only the most superficial part of identification, in this case with the father. And, according to him, this identification is of a symbolic order – although here Lacan does not tell us in what sense this "acting like the father" corresponds to a symbolic position. What Anna Freud describes in terms of processes (of action and reaction), Lacan sees in terms of structure.

We also notice, however, that though here Lacan criticizes the way in which Anna interprets the case – her metapsychological, I would call it, language, geared towards the analysis of defences and resistances – he by no means disputes the reconstruction offered by Anna Freud, who is honest enough to say that she was mistaken at first, that she immediately wanted to include in the transference tactic something much more original that merely repeated itself in transference: a paternal ideal of a sarcastic disengagement from the emotions. Lacan does not actually dispute Anna Freud's analytical technique; he disputes the conceptual framework with which she reads what is happening. His criticism therefore appears, if not too harsh, at least a little excessive. And it certainly perplexes us that, as he did in Kris's case, Lacan convinces himself that he knows what actually happened better than the analyst who is bringing the case.

Notes

1 Anna Freud, 1946, pp. 35–37.
2 Grosskurth, 1986, p. 251.

Chapter 20

The Freudian Legacy

In the same session (Chapter 6) in which he analyses Anna Freud's case, Lacan also analyses a case published by Melanie Klein, that of the boy called little Dick. Today we would diagnose Dick as a child on the autistic spectrum, but at that time autism, though it had already been described by Kanner and Asperger few years earlier, had not become part of a diagnostic routine. Today we would say that Klein acts as if he had been a psychotic child, but autism is not psychosis.[1] However, we shall not comment here on the Lacanian commentary of the case.

The comparison between Anna Freud and Klein seems to be to the latter's advantage. In short, according to Lacan, Klein is closer to the original spirit of Freudian analysis (a conclusion that Klein herself probably would not have shared). A meticulous analysis of the Lacanian commentary, however, would lead us to different conclusions: Lacan openly indicates what he perceives as the limits of the Kleinian approach, which he accuses of a certain – and he repeats the concept several times – "brutality" ("*instinct de brute*") and even defines as "revolting" (*Se1*, 81–2).

Lacan dares to express what many think when reading M. Klein: her rush to interpret. Reading Klein's clinical cases, we have the impression that she undertakes a kind of consecutive translation in Unconscian, indeed a Kleinish language of everything the subject says or does. Everything is constantly interpreted in a Kleinian key. For example:

"Little Dick makes his little toy train enter the tunnel"
means
"Dick's father's penis is penetrating his mother"

Compared to this frantic need to interpret everything immediately, Anna Freud and the ego psychologists' dwelling on the surface seems more convincing. Many rightly prefer the latter, also because it seems closer to Sigmund's clinical style.

I'm not saying that one should overthrow Lacan's preferences and opt for the Anna-Freudian clinical approach. Probably every analytic school has the two poles, on the one hand the rush to interpret and on the other working close to the surface and to the here-and-now. They are two ways – the former paradigmatic, the latter syntagmatic – of approaching the clinical thing.

DOI: 10.4324/9781003388098-20

To return to Lacan, one may suspect that his preference for Klein at the time was not so strongly felt and probably due to politics within the IPA. Anna Freud and Klein were entirely alternative, and it was necessary to side with one or the other in order to play the game, even if siding with Klein was not at all a wise political move at that time, given the context of his Société française de psychanalyse, as we have seen.

Lacan knew that Anna Freud clearly disliked him; moreover, Anna was friends with Princess Marie Bonaparte, who was his declared enemy in France. (Did Lacan know that Marie Bonaparte had also been the mistress of Löwenstein, his analyst?) This pushed him to lean in favour of Klein. Lacan and Klein met at the 16th IPA congress in Zurich in 1949. It seems that on first contact Klein was impressed with Lacan. He tried to form an alliance with her by proposing to translate her essay *The Psychoanalysis of Children*, published in 1932, from the German into French; Klein gladly accepted.

Back in Paris, Lacan assigned the translation to his patient and pupil René Diatkine, who translated the first part of the text and gave it to Lacan without thinking of keeping a copy for himself. In August 1951, at the Amsterdam congress, Melanie learned from Diatkine that the translation of the first part of her essay was his. That autumn, it is not clear why, Lacan proposed to the French Kleinian analyst Françoise Boulanger and her husband that they might translate the second part of *The Psychoanalysis of Children* from the English (why resort to other translators? Was he dissatisfied with Diatkine's translation?). Boulanger and her husband began translating the text, but when they asked Lacan for the first part already translated in order to harmonize the two texts, they found that Lacan had lost the French version and that Diatkine had not kept a copy. Lacan was careful not to mention this to Klein. The fact is that, in January 1952, the Boulangers told Klein the story. Now, not only did Lacan fail to reveal that he had lost the Diatkine translation, but he never officially admitted it either. This clearly discredited Lacan in Klein's eyes, and she eventually steered clear of him.[2]

Losing a text is a parapraxis that demands an interpretation. In other words, deep down Lacan had no desire to publish Klein's text, even though she could have been a strategic ally. Lacan ultimately realized that Klein was by no means interested in his thought. The truth is that neither was interested in the other's work and that their alliance was simply tactical: "the enemy of my enemy is my friend". Still, in 1954 Lacan could entertain some hope of an alliance with Klein, so he treated her relatively well in this seminar. But he devotes far more space – with no shortage of criticism – to the thought of Michael Balint, who was certainly no Kleinian; he too was a Londoner of Hungarian origin. And Balint was also in many ways opposed to Kleinian theses. In any case, once the possibility of an alliance with the Kleinians had faded, Lacan would only rarely refer to Klein and her doctrines.

But why should someone who in France proclaimed a "return to Freud" have attempted an association with Melanie Klein? Freud had pronounced himself against Klein's ideas in private by supporting his daughter Anna. To go against Freud's opinion, even after his death, was not the most credible way to proclaim yourself a

Freudian. What evidently played a role in Lacan's – aborted – choice was the dislike Anna Freud and Marie Bonaparte had for him. But I believe there was a more profound reason: that his real adversaries were precisely those, like Anna, who declared themselves Freudians and legitimate heirs of Freud's thought. Klein, well beforehand, had set herself apart from the Freudian lineage, and indeed in Britain the gap between Freudians and Kleinians would widen more and more. Since Lacan's secret desire was to pose as Freud's true heir, his authentic rivals were clearly the Freudians.

For a long while, to say "Freudians" in Britain did not distinguish between generic Freudians and those who followed in the footsteps of Anna – an identification that by no means applied in France or in other Latin countries. Nobody in Italy identifies Anna Freud with her father's thought; the (very few) Anna-Freudians are clearly distinguished from Freudians. And, in contrast to the United States, in France and Italy, Anna Freud has always been considered a minor analyst.

This continuity with Freud – the idea of being to Freud what Paul of Tarsus was to Jesus, his apostle – is stressed by Lacan's terminological choices. When he founded his school in 1963 he called it École Freudienne, and not École de psychanalyse. And even when he eventually dissolved the École in 1980, Lacan planned to found a new society, La Cause Freudienne. The appeal to Freud was more important to him than the appeal to psychoanalysis. Evidently, his sharp opposition to Freud's "legitimate" daughter had more than a political meaning: it was a conflict between two symbolic lineages.

And it is in this key that we should read his violent opposition to Kris: not simply because Kris was a supporter of Anna Freud, but because he was a kind of symbolic twin of his. The same age as he, Kris belonged to the second generation of Freudians. Just like him, Kris drew directly on Freud's teaching but setting forth a technical innovation – the primacy of analysis of defences. And Lacan himself was a proponent of a technical innovation – the use of variable time in sessions. Both Kris and Lacan represented a reforming continuity with regard to their father Freud. It therefore appeared essential for Lacan to counter the ramifications of ego psychology in order to affirm himself as the legitimate heir of Freud but also as the only credible innovator at the technical level. This is why he dedicated his first seminar to "The Technical Writings of Freud".

The following year he entitled his seminar "The Ego in Freud's Theory and in the Technique of Psychoanalysis". Here too what seemed to him to be a priority at the time was to oppose the ego psychologists by proposing his own alternative view both of analytical technique and of the Ego according to Freud. From 1955 onwards, however, this opposition ceased to interest him, as did his contentious attitude towards other analysts in general. More and more rarely would he enter into conflict with other analytic approaches.

Notes

1 I argue that one should not confuse autism with psychosis in Benvenuto (2019, 2020). This separation is not at all accepted by mainstream Lacanians.
2 See Roudinesco, 1992, pp. 265–266.

Chapter 21

Interpretation and Truth

What essentially is Lacan's "technical" criticism of Kris, this rebuke that becomes more and more severe with the passage of time? That it is basically pointless to make the subject recognize a realistic truth.

We know that with psychotics to tell the objective truth is more than simply pointless but a positively harmful intervention. *Always Tell Him "Yes"* is the title of a well-known Italian play by Eduardo De Filippo that depicts a psychotic: "Heaven forbid anyone contradicting him! He'd hate us if we did". If a paranoid person says "the neighbours are spying on me!", never say "Look, you're wrong, I can prove to you that nobody is spying on you!" He would probably be outraged and retort: "Are you saying I'm paranoid?" With a patient like Brain[1] – Lacan seems to be saying – Kris will not elicit a furious response but an acting out, as if he said: "What do I care if I don't really plagiarize, the important thing is that *I want to* devour other people's brains!" For Lacan, the analysis of defences – although it had been advocated by Freud – is a naive appeal to an objective reality that has no value for unconscious life. It would be like saying to a fetishist: "Look, women don't have a penis, you have to desire them without the fetish!"; the fetishist will not stop desiring women insofar as they have a mock penis.

But is this entirely true?

There are situations in which the admission of a reality, or non-reality, of a belief is the *sine qua non* of an analysis. Take the case of hypochondriac, who consult a hundred doctors to discover what their illness might be, but, test after test, nothing shows up. For as long as a hypochondriac remains convinced that the only point in question is finally finding the correct medical diagnosis, he or she will not consult a psychotherapist. When a hypochondriac becomes resigned to meeting a therapist, this is already facing up to the evidence, however negative, that the disorder is not related to an organic lesion. Yet a hypochondriac who agrees to undergo an analytical process remains divided, admitting on the one hand the "psychological", so to speak, nature of the illness and on the other remaining anchored to its organic reality, a cherished reality, one that seems to be a point of honour, a way of presenting him- or herself as the victim of an obscure evil that eludes all scientific knowledge.

But if analysts should never pose as witnesses or guarantors of reality, as Lacan thinks, what then is their function? To interpret. But to interpret the need to

DOI: 10.4324/9781003388098-21

plagiarize already means *ipso facto* to deny the reality of the plagiarism. In fact, Brain does not say "I have an awful craving to plagiarize others". He says: "I have a compulsion to plagiarize others"; that is, he locates his desire to plagiarize in the *act* of plagiarizing; he describes himself as almost unaware of his plagiarizing in the same way as the hypochondriac situates his or her "*être mal dans sa peau*", feeling unwell in one's skin, in the reality of his or her body as persecutory Other. It would seem, in short, that what counts for Lacan is interpreting the unconscious drive, not rectifying the subject's relation to the real (though he had himself indicated the latter as the end of analysis). Interpretation is not rectification. Yet he takes it for granted that there is a rectification at the end of the process. If the result of Brain's analysis was positive, as Kris claims, this can only mean not that Brain stopped plagiarizing but that Brain stopped *believing he plagiarizes*.

Lacan's criticism of Kris's efforts to make the patient recognize reality certainly goes in the direction of de-intellectualizing analytical practice. Those who do not really know Lacan believe, on the contrary, that he aims at intellectualizing psychoanalysis, given the profusion of his learned references and the minor role – so they believe – that he gives to affects. In actual fact, Lacan seeks to detach analytic effectiveness from any purely conceptual clarification; he does not believe that the meaning of what an analyst says really acts on analysands. For this reason, at least at an early stage, Lacan prefers interpretations based essentially on the signifier, that is, on the rebus, the quip, the pun . . . as Freud often did, though not systematically. Insisting on the signifier seemed to him a more concrete way of affecting the unconscious. In this way he brought into psychoanalysis the project of the great artistic avant-gardes of the 20th century, which suspend or erase meaning to focus on the signifier.

It must be said, however, that over time Lacan increasingly reduced interpretive intervention. The impression is that what ultimately counted for Lacan was the act of interrupting the session: the interpretative value lies in *when* an analyst puts an end to a session (not an astronomical "when" but a logical "when": that is, in the temporality intrinsic to the analysand's speech). As we have seen, interpretation basically coincides with an acting. But this is nevertheless done on the analysand's speech; it is indeed an acting, but on the signifier itself.

A vast issue opens up here, one that we can only sketch out but that lies at the core of the essence of analytical practice and its survival: the role of interpretation in an analytic relationship. It is usually said that the analyst intervenes in two ways: by managing transference and by interpreting. But other psychotherapies also deal with transference, albeit differently, whereas what really makes analyses an analysis and not a psychotherapy is precisely the use of interpretation.

Yet the tendency of many schools of psychoanalysis is more and more to forego interpretations, simply because they present "concepts" and they are not acts. In fact, it's quite striking how many analysands with a good knowledge of psychoanalytic literature continually resort to "good interpretations" and metapsychological concepts, often quite correctly, precisely as a weapon to shut down their unconscious. It's a way of intellectualizing analytical work, effectively demolishing its impact. Hence the idea that, rather than interpreting, what really matters is the analyst's handling of transference. In this way analysis can bring about change insofar as it acts on the subjective relationship between analyst and analysand – this thesis derives from an influential essay by Strachey (1934).[2] In other words, interpretation risks being an intellectual mask disguising what really *occurs* in analysis, namely a conversion in the way of being with others. In short, the analyst is a kind of surrogate object that allows the analysand to modify profoundly her or his relationship with others; hence the preponderance of the intersubjectivist vision, according to which analysis is a rectification of our way of communicating. *Dasein* (being-there) resolves itself entirely in *Mitsein* (being-with).

Even the most steadfast analyst admits that psychotherapists of other schools and trends can fulfil reconversion work on a par with analysis. They will admit that transference can be established not only with an analyst but with shrinks of any other school as well. So, if what ultimately counts is transference and not so much what the psychotherapist says or does, in what does the *specific* effectiveness of analysis consist? This would lead us to the conclusion that in fact the analytic apparatus is a theoretical superstructure of an act of cure that can be performed by anyone, even a cognitive behavioural psychologist.

The truth is that the great appeal of psychoanalysis, especially among intellectuals, has always been its claim to *curing through truth*. It applies the evangelical motto *veritas vos liberat*, "truth will set you free".[3] Not mere pragmatic effectiveness but the actual strength of a revelation about what is – *what* I really desire – distinguishes psychoanalysis from most of other psychotherapeutic strategies. (Lacan calls this "what I desire" object *a*. But he himself states that this object cannot be *said*. Yet analysis is only effective to the extent that it modifies the subject's relation to object *a*. But if this new relation cannot be said and yet *happens*, the role of the speech – which Lacan glorifies – is ultimately rather marginal. The speech, then, as Lacan himself will say, is a *semblant*, a semblance. Analytical interpretation itself is therefore *semblant*. Hence the strong temptation, even among Lacanians, to abandon interpretation.) But to reveal this truth, it must somehow be *said*. Truth is a function of saying, not so much said by the analyst as by the analysand: it is necessary to bring the subject to tell the truth ("the full speech", *la parole pleine*). Now, interpretation is valuable for psychoanalysis only to the extent that it is correct. Psychoanalysis counts on the fact that not every interpretation is valid, but only *certain* interpretations are. But if the role of interpretations is reduced to the point of disappearing, or if every interpretation is as good as another, we could come to the conclusion that anyone could occupy the place of the analyst.

As is often the case, it is artists who sense, more than analysts and theorists, the truly important issues. Several films deal with subjects treated and cured by non-analysts. In Patrice Leconte's film *Confidences trop intimes* (*Intimate Strangers*, 2004), for example, a young woman goes to see an analyst for the first time, but she finds the wrong door and ends up in an accountant's office. She speaks to him as someone would to an analyst, and the accountant is dumbfounded. By the time the misunderstanding is cleared up, however, a transference has already been established between the two. The accountant consults the analyst on his landing, who advises him to continue the analysis himself. This eventually has a positive outcome . . . with the "analyst" and "patient" marrying. And I could mention other popular works of fiction in which an analysis is conducted by a false analyst whom the patient believes to be an authentic one.[4] Moral of the story: even an accountant can be a good analyst, as long as the right transference is established.

But in this way, as we have said, analysis turns into a psychotherapy like any other. And the tendency of much psychoanalysis today is to dissolve itself into psychotherapy, that is, in a logotherapy where the cure is not based on telling the truth.

On the one hand we have a hermeneutic psychoanalysis for which one interpretation is as good as another as long as subjects construct, with the analyst's help, a happy narrative. Not a true narrative, but a happy one, or rather, true insofar as it is happy. Within this perspective, interpretation loses any value of truth; the important thing is for subjects to tell themselves *the happy story*. On the other hand, there is a psychoanalysis that relinquishes any interpretative work and focuses everything on the "analyst-analysand relationship", on the intersubjective dynamics between the two. In this view, in the wake of Heinz Kohut, what really counts is empathy on the part of the analyst. Empathy is at the basis of any friendly relationship, so in fact analysis boils down to a successful relationship between two friends. Anyone is capable of empathy towards another person, even an accountant.

As we can see, in both cases psychoanalysis forgoes its original ambition: curing by appealing to truth – to a truth that may not be spoken but which must show itself somehow. Yet the whole future of psychoanalysis will be played out in the wake of this ambition.

Notes

1 Although the diagnosis remains uncertain, since Lacan, as we have seen, hypothesizes an oral foreclosure. The evocation of foreclosure suggests something of the psychotic.
2 J. Strachey wondered which interpretations were "mutative", that is, effective, coming to the conclusion that these were the transferential interpretations. Effectiveness lies in interpreting the *hic et nunc* of the relationship. This idea would become dominant in mainstream psychoanalysis.
3 John 8:32.
4 Another good example is *Matchstick Men* by Ridley Scott (2003).

Chapter 22

Laughing Unconscious

Though Lacan's critical reinterpretation of Anna Freud's case comes across as a little far fetched, one thing is clear: Lacan rejects Anna's view of subjectivity. The discussion of technique is a light veil that only vaguely conceals Lacan's true aim: to reject ego psychology's conception of subjectivity.

The Anna-Freudian and ego-psychological vision is based on a military, as I would call it, figure of the ego: the ego is like a fortress or a castle that needs constantly to defend itself from attacks and strikes on three fronts. It needs to fend off attacks from the internal drives, from moral self-reproaches and from external pressures. The insistence on defences and resistances gives a besieged and threatened image of the ego, which appears as a permanent swordsman engaged in combat. Although this image of the ego is also to be found in Sigmund Freud, Lacan in fact appeals to another unconscious: the one that emerges in Freud's essay *Jokes and Their Relation to the Unconscious* (Freud, 1905a). And in fact Lacan dedicates part of his 1957 seminar to this essay.[1]

Freudians usually consider this essay by Freud a minor work and point out that Freud did not return to the subject after its publication. On the contrary, for Lacan this work is one of the pillars of the Freudian conception. Lacan makes wit, humour, one of the fundamental *formations of the unconscious* – the others being dreams, neurotic and psychotic symptoms and parapraxes. Now, wit possesses one singular characteristic compared to the other formations of the unconscious: that it is always a source of pleasure. If successful, it makes us laugh. Dreams can be pleasant, but they can be nightmares too, while witticisms, if they hit the right note, are always pleasant. In short, the unconscious is not only a source of distress and threats: it is also a form of enjoyment. The eminent position Lacan gives to jokes makes explicit, albeit obliquely, his vision of the unconscious: that it is not only the seat of repression, of that which needs to be suppressed and always resurfaces, but it is also an agency of creative transgression. It is the libidinal force on which a subject can draw in order to express something new, something not predetermined, not put in a cast. The unconscious for Lacan is first and foremost the fact that, even if unbeknownst to us, it (*es*) enjoys.

Take one of the examples Freud gives, taken from Heine: the poor Jew Hirsch Hyacinthe meets Rothschild, an extremely rich Jew, and says that the latter treated

DOI: 10.4324/9781003388098-22

him *famillionairely*, fusing the words "familiar" and "millionaire" (Freud, 1905a, p. 12). Now, if we conceive of the unconscious "strictly" as the place of the repressed, the forgotten, we wonder what the unconscious has to do with the creation of this neologism, "famillionairely". What of the repressed is resurfacing in this pun?

Evidently, here Freud is proposing, however indirectly, a broader conception of the unconscious than is usually perceived: here the unconscious is a kind of source of creativity, and, in the case of the *Witz*, of a peculiar creativity that coincides with a transgression: that is, *taking the liberty of amusing oneself with language*. It is as if we all spoke with an unwritten clause that binds and disciplines us, "respect language! Remember that it is denotative, referential!" In the same way that God's name must not be taken in vain, language too should not be taken in vain. Instead, a *Witz* like *famillionairely* produces a partly stolen pleasure, not entirely licit, let's call it, because it says and doesn't say; it manipulates the signifier to derive from it a "not much sense" that to us also comes across as a "more sense". In short, for Lacan the unconscious is also a restless playing with the signifier, and humour is a compliant masturbation of language.

The unconscious is a transgression to which the ego responds not only with repression, with the *Abwehr*, avoidance or defence, but with disinhibition too. Laughter is the manifestation of a disinhibition. The Lacanian unconscious, though undoubtedly connected to repression, occupies a vaster area than the repressed alone: something from it invades us and diverts us from a fixation, from a kind of rigidity. Hence Lacan's dislike for Anna Freud, her followers and their vision, which I have called a military vision of subjectivity. For Lacan, the model of subjectivity of so many of Freud's students who emigrated mainly to Britain and America is that of the renegade Jew who had to adapt to a foreign and often hostile world. The Lacanian model of the unconscious, on the other hand, is that of the libertine or the dandy, whose aim it is to transgress in order to find enjoyment. These two visions also represent two entirely different ethics of subjectivity.

It is this core ethical difference that authentically separates Lacan from Anna Freud, Kris and the other ego-psychologists. But evidently the clinical material they offered him was totally inadequate to bring out this partly latent difference: after all, these analysts that he criticizes remain Freudians. Hence the need to misinterpret (even overwhelmingly, as we've seen) Kris's text and also a somewhat malicious way of reading the case brought by Anna Freud. In short, Lacan sought in clinical practice a difference that lay elsewhere: in a different philosophical vision of human subjectivity. A difference that needed to be given *clinical substance*.

Note

1 Se5, chapters I–VII.

Chapter 23

Reformatory Analysis

Ego psychology takes the concept of "Ego" from Freud's "structural model", as it is referred to in English (Ego, Id and Super-Ego), making it the instance that the analyst should promote: the aim of analysis is to strengthen the Ego as a desexualized conflict-free area so as to adapt it to external reality and allow it to adjust optimally to the social demands of the environment

We will not dwell here on the mostly scathing criticisms Lacan lavished on this approach, criticisms that Herbert Marcuse formulated at about the same time in a not entirely dissimilar fashion. We shall limit ourselves here to marking the essentially ethical point of his opposition to Kris.

For instance, here he scoffs at Kris's use of the term "pattern of behaviour": "we clearly see that the analysis of the subject's behaviour patterns amounts to inscribing his behaviour in the analyst's patterns" (*E I*, 394–5), This too, however, is an unfair criticism. What Kris calls "patterns of behaviour" seem to be what we would call *repetitions in acting*. We call neurotic those people who tend to always behave in the same way in certain situations, to repeat what they did in the past, which usually represented a major blow. It's what gives every neurotic's life a peculiar mark, that of being someone who never learns from experience. This seems to be the "pattern" according to Kris. And it seems to me to correspond to what Lacan ascribes to the *phantasme* (imago) of the subject, which structures much of its behaviour. I do not see any attempt by Kris to make the patient's behaviour fall under the pattern – the imago – of the analyst.

Pattern is an English term that is undoubtedly difficult to translate into French. Its meaning can therefore drift from one language to another. (Kris probably wanted to express in English what in German is referred to as *Gestalt*.) If we compare what Kris writes with what Edward Bibring, whom he quotes, said,[1] we can in fact see that this pattern is very similar to Lacan's *phantasme* (another term that's difficult to translate), which is not so much a structure but more precisely a pattern.

In any case, Lacan raises a problem that goes far beyond being a critique of ego psychology and its clinical stratagems: the manipulative tendency of much too much psychoanalysis, in wanting to correct the behaviours and ways of life of patients in order to reshape them in the image and likeness of the behaviours and ways of life that the analyst considers positive, psychologically correct, that

DOI: 10.4324/9781003388098-23

is, his own. I have seen myself how this manipulative tendency is also present in Lacanian analysts, because the temptation is too strong for anyone who is given the position of healer – a position that often slides into pedagogy.

Analysts sometimes find themselves (like Kris in the case we're examining) seeing analysands who had previous experiences with other analysts or psychotherapists from different schools, and they're often the source of some ludicrous stories. We should never take what analysands say about their former analysts literally, because more often than not analysands entirely misunderstand their analysts' words. (Do so many of the things we say to our analysands that produce very positive effects fail to work because they are misunderstood?) But it's quite striking how the attitude of many Lacanian colleagues actually goes in an openly normative direction, flouting the principles established by Lacan himself. And it makes us wonder: *is it ultimately possible for an analyst, of whatever background, to avoid an implicit set of norms that often elude the consciousness of the analyst himself?* Is there not a normative implication in every transference? We very often impose norms on others silently; prescriptions are mostly unconscious. What if the analyst's absolute neutrality were a pure legend, an ideal that cannot be achieved in this world?

Lacan is particularly harsh towards the criterion according to which the aim of analytic treatment is to make the patient introject the Ego of the analyst ("I hope that here, in fact, they mean to talk about the healthy part [of the analyst's Ego]", he comments ironically). According to this approach, the analyst proposes his own Ego as their patient's attainable ideal and hence analysis as a re-educational process in the broadest sense, in which the analyst uses a position of prestige to mould the psyche of the patient-pupil according to what the analyst-master considers ideal for a subject.

Now, it so happens that after dwelling on Prof. Brain's case, Kris, in the same article, gives us the broad outlines of another case. A patient suffered from certain symptoms, "particularly prolonged states of sexual excitement, interrupted but hardly alleviated by compulsive masturbation or its equivalents, which in some cases led to disguised impulses toward exhibitionism" (Kris, 1951, p. 27). Let us leave aside how Kris reconstructs this state of chronic excitement and what he draws from it. The crux is: in what sense can we consider prolonged states of sexual arousal symptoms? That is, what is a symptom in psychoanalysis?

In medicine the symptom is the trace of an underlying morbid process, in short, of an illness, whereas in psychoanalysis the symptom is the "morbid" process itself: it is a sign of something that is not properly morbid in itself. Usually anything about us that is ego-dystonic, that is, that makes us suffer for one reason or another and that we do not accept, is considered a symptom. (In the case of perversions, I would rather speak of *hetero-dystonia*, in the case of psychoses of *socio-dystonia*.[2] But what we are inclined to brand as "pathological" is always a dystonia.)

The point is that what we consider ego-dystonic is in fact such above all because it is also socio-dystonic; that is, it puts us in an uncomfortable social position. Decades ago in America there were analysts and psychiatrists who treated homosexuality; today a treatment of this kind would be unthinkable (although it is practised within Protestant religious communities, such as the Evangelicals). This is because back then homosexuality was considered a pathological symptom; today it has been decided that it is no longer that. The DSM, the *Diagnostic and Statistical Manual of Mental Disorders*, has not included homosexuality as a mental disorder since 1974. At that time there was much more pain in being homosexual – homosexual orientation was therefore very egodystonic – because that way of desiring was socially frowned upon.

What, on the other hand, is to be said of someone who is prey to sexual arousal to a degree and frequency far above average? Is deviating from a statistical average, not being in the middle of a Gaussian curve, of a "normal distribution", a symptom? Kinsey said that "a woman is a nymphomaniac when she has more sex than you do".

Of course, being sexually aroused all the time is not comfortable, but is it enough to consider certain impulses unpleasant to consider them symptoms? Certainly not everything that we dislike about ourselves is a symptom, but nor is it certain that what psychoanalysis considers a symptom is something we dislike about ourselves. As a matter of fact, the consideration of the symptom among analysts oscillates between a utilitarian conception that decrees morbid anything that is inconvenient for the subject (Would then tending to fatness or having a low IQ be symptoms in need of treatment?) and a more refined one, according to which the symptom is a sign of a psychic conflict and therefore of an "alienation". But in this case Kris – by accepting as a symptom the fact that the subject is displeased with the excess of his own libido – does not problematize the concept of symptom at all. And the symptom is one of the most elusive – and most fundamental – concepts in psychoanalysis.

Similar considerations should also apply to other syndromes, for example, attention-deficit hyperactive disorder (ADHD). I can appreciate that having a child with ADHD in a school classroom is something dramatic for a teacher, but the point is: is it also something dramatic for the child with child? Do we not all try to amuse ourselves, to distract ourselves, from what bores us?

When I was in primary school, I often found lessons extremely boring, despite being the best in the class. So, I perfectly understood my classmate Bruzzese, someone who today would be labelled today as having ADHD. He would often make lewd comments, which the teacher didn't approve of at all, or stand up from his desk without permission, and in fact poor Bruzzese was repeatedly slapped in the face (something a teacher could do back then). Often, however, his wisecracks made us laugh, and we objected to the angry reactions of our teacher, who felt his authority being threatened. Bruzzese was actually a very intelligent, sincere and amiable child, albeit rather over the top. He refused to accept school rules, which the rest of us, however tedious we found them, endured. In short, ADHD is for the most part a socio-dystonia. But *what is it a symptom of*? In psychiatry, symptoms are symptoms of a syndrome that amounts to the set of symptoms in themselves.

Today ego psychology is undergoing a crisis; it has lost the predominant position it held back then, in the 1950s. The generalized crisis of psychoanalysis in America has struck ego psychology hardest. Historically, Lacan – and all those who attacked ego psychology, such as the Kleinians – ultimately won their battle. Is then Lacan's controversy outdated today? Not entirely.

At present, most (non-Lacanian) analysts regard analysis as a kind of "second opportunity" of growth offered to the patient: they take it as a matter of fact that patients had unhappy childhoods, that their mothers were not "good enough", hence all their problems. The mother is almost always to blame for everything (the father's function has almost disappeared in current psychoanalysis). Analysis is essentially taken to be a sort of second childhood "upon appeal", brought to life in the analytic kindergarten in order to correct the first childhood: the analyst tries to function as a supplementary corrective mother. I should say that this is what analysis basically amounts to for 90% of analysts. But even here, analysts, by identifying their position with that of a mother, albeit one of second instance, are in fact attributing to themselves a purely nurturing and edifying function. A sentimental education but an education in any case. Psychoanalysis, having ceased to see itself as a medical psychotherapy, has been largely sucked into a "formative" ideal of a maternal pedagogical nature. At the time Kris wrote his article, the analyst's fundamental identification was with the psychiatrist (albeit one in a suit and tie, not in a white coat). Today, the paradigmatic identification of analysts is to caring kindergarten teachers. Over time, psychoanalysis seems to have fallen from the medical frying pan into the re-educational furnace.

Lacan's school was the most drastic attempt to separate psychoanalytic practice not only from medical psychotherapy but also from educational, formative and re-formative strategies. Obviously, we need to ask ourselves to what extent this purification and empowerment of psychoanalysis – freed of any medical and pedagogical dross – is practicable *de facto*: to what extent, in other words, it won't become guilty of a *hybris* of purity, or utopia.

Lacan's ethical choice – quite astonishing for such a sound liberal – to instead consider the Ego (*le moi*) the true foe and refuse to reinforce it should instead be read in the context of the specific *ethos* of French intellectuality, particularly the Parisian, an *ethos* that even here should be considered from the political point of view. Though a very prestigious Marxist-Leninist intelligentsia had been developing in France for decades, the philosophical genome – as we say today – of the French *intellectuel* is anarchism. Sartre himself admitted that his Marxist allegiance was a way of making his own underlying passionate anarchism culturally respectable.[3] An anarchist tradition that would then express itself sharply and compellingly in Michel Foucault, Gilles Deleuze and many others. The non-conservative French intellectual is much closer to the anarchism of Sade, the Surrealists, Georges Sorel, Bataille and Foucault than to the socialist technocracy of the *enarques* (the alumni of the ENA, the *École Normale d'Administration*, the Grande Ecole that produces much of the French ruling class, particularly the political one). In short, French intellectuality deeply loathes the state even more – and more authentically – than it abhors capitalism. Significantly therefore, the most important French Marxist thinker, Louis Althusser (2014), was notable for his analysis of the "ideological State Apparatuses". For French intellectuals, the state is a huge ideological force, stronger than the Catholic church and free-market theory; the state is horrifying. In this, the French intelligentsia seems akin to American free-market conservatives, for whom distrust of the state and its controls is paramount.

Yet the underlying anarchism of the *intellectuels* somehow extols a type of anarchism that seems to me to be the fundamental character of Western culture (not mass culture, of course) in the 20th century. In art, in philosophy, in psychoanalysis . . . the thought of the last century was marked by an anarchic rejection of any hierarchies and authoritarianisms. The adherence of many intellectuals to Marxism or Leninism was in fact a mask to give "scientific" respectability to a basic ethical option: freedom from any pre-established hierarchy. Lacan's work and practice should be seen in this purely 20th-century perspective.

In this context of anarchism, the Freudian Ego was soon identified, and not only by Lacan, with the state and its administrative apparatuses. Each subject became a sort of political body, with a population pushing for its demands (the Id), with an institutional apparatus of laws and regulations (the Superego) and with a government (the Ego) that has to mediate between the two. To paraphrase the American republican motto Reagan voiced ("Government is not the solution to our problem, government is the problem"), Lacan basically says "the Ego is not the solution, the Ego is the problem".

One need only think of the man Lacan. He steered clear of public institutions such as the universities, the hospital system, the psycho-pedagogical institutions, the French Grandes Écoles and so on. He only ever pursued a radically liberal, freelance profession and ended up breaking with the only institution – albeit a private one – that had embraced him: the IPA. Of course, he then founded his own institution, the École Freudienne, but it was characterized by a minimalist bureaucracy – more than compensated for by its charismatic anarchist master – who ended up alienating some of his less libertarian students (the split of the so-called Fourth Group of analysts in 1969).[4] Of course, many Lacanians have occupied a prominent place in state institutions, but I would say always with a sort of guilty conscience. They justified their being within an institution as "spreading the plague in the apparatuses of the state", somewhat like the legend spread by Lacan himself, according to which Freud said to Jung upon arriving in America in 1909: "These Americans don't know that we are bringing them the plague!"

Of course, we cannot live without the state or without the Ego, but we can try to dodge them through *evasion*. Not in the sense of tax evasion or entertainment but evasion towards spheres not controlled by the state/Ego. The Ego is a mechanism for dodging whatever tends to disintegrate; anarchism, even of the existential kind, is a dodging of the dodging mechanism. It is a form of *evasione*, in the triple sense that the term has in the Italian language (tax evasion, escaping from prison and entertainment).

Initially, for Lacan, it was necessary to dodge the ego-state in order to practise what he called the "Full Word". Why did he choose the term *full*? What vacuity should we avoid? The vacuity is precisely that of legal words, the words we should utter, the "fine words" we should use if we want to do things correctly. The fullness Lacan aims for is instead the fact that the word should let itself be completely penetrated by life. At least at an early stage, to the small and wise economies of the Ego Lacan ethically opposed what phenomenology called *Lebenswelt*, life world.

As we said, a good part of Lacan's success is due to his systematic and ingenious subversion of all common psychological beliefs, thus revealing them as kitsch. Our current view of the mind leads us to see the Ego as the instance that controls our irrational, and therefore dangerous, impulses. If I'm angry with my wife and threaten her with a knife, it is evidently the Id (It) expressing itself, but the Ego tells me that I must not do such a thing, not least because if I really did kill her, I'd end up in jail. The Ego seems to bring us back to reality, to what best suits us, to our "advantage", which corresponds to what we consider wise for us and for others. In short, the Freudian Ego seems to be the new name given to the sort of reason that restrains our non-reflective instincts, an essentially positive instance, since, according to tradition, the human being is an *animal rationale*; were it not so, the human being would be just animal.

Lacan overturns all this: in his system the Ego becomes, if not an evil instance, certainly the agent of that utilitarian calculation that removes our unconscious drives. But then, would I have been better off stabbing my wife without heeding the wise counsels of my ego? Lacan cannot go that far. Rather, he would say that hatred for my wife does not pass through speech and is expressed by acting out, precisely because the Ego has not allowed this hatred access to speech and thus to symbolic processing. By obstructing the unconscious, the Ego allows it to run rampant in harmful and self-destructive acts.

Notes

1 Kris (1951, p. 24 n) quotes Waelder: "Bibring speaks of 'singling out' a patient's present pattern of behavior and arriving, by way of a large number of immediate patterns, at the original pattern. The present pattern embodies the instinctual impulses and anxieties now operative, as well as the ego's present methods of elaboration (some of which are stereotyped responses to impulses and anxieties which have ceased to exist)".
2 I expanded on these differences in Benvenuto, 2016, chapter 1.
3 See Louette, 2006.
4 Quatrième Groupe, Organisation psychanalytique de langue française (OPLF), founded by Piera Aulagnier, François Perrier and Jean-Paul Valabrega. It is still in existence and is chaired by Eric Julliand.

Chapter 24

Adaptive Analysis

In psychoanalysis today we're far removed from the 1950s, a time when the afore-mentioned diatribes were taking place. During that decade there was a powerful struggle within the IPA – and Lacan was then a budding IPA analyst – for a Freudian *legitimization*. As in 4th-century theological disputes, when it was a matter of clearly marking the distance between Christian orthodoxy and heresies, at the time it seemed essential to define the boundaries of a *good psychoanalysis* versus the bad varieties or anything that was unlawfully passed off as psychoanalysis. Lacan's violent attack on ego psychology is null today, when an extremely smooth and cool pluralism prevails. Each school of thought pursues its work within its paradigm and rarely attacks the other schools. Some schools ignore each other, some mutually take cues and adopt elements from each other, but on the whole the struggle for analytical legitimacy is over. So, our reconstruction of the Lacan–Anna Freud–Kris conflict has the flavour of a retro world and era. But it is important to understand this little ancient world in order to also understand the conflicts and squabbles of the not much bigger modern world.

Today, the various psychoanalytic approaches – not to mention all the other psy-chotherapies that generically refer to psychoanalysis – do not pose themselves as excelling the others on the basis of a criterion of correctness. The question is not conducting the most correct analysis, one closer to the spirit, if not to the letter, of what Freud performed or wrote. It seems to me that today the various approaches compete in the broader market of "psycho-treatments" by appealing either to greater therapeutic effectiveness or to greater perspicuity. The Lacanians, in particular, do not propose themselves as more therapeutically effective but as more perspicuous: they think of themselves as coming closer to the truth of the unconscious.

For decades researchers have been carrying out comparative studies on the responsive effectiveness of the various psychotherapeutic techniques, and the general feeling is that the results are rather chaotic.[1] These comparative empirical studies clash with the heterogeneity of what each technique considers "successful" in a treatment. A patient may come into analysis complaining of a certain symptom, which may be eliminated within a few sessions: yet the subject continues the analy-sis for years, since by then his demand for cure has changed. Can we say that this analysis was a success because it cured the subject's complaint in a short time or

DOI: 10.4324/9781003388098-24

a failure because the subject continues to return to analysis for years? Therapeutic success is not an event external to the strategies and theoretical framework of the various psychotherapies, but is a constituent part of them: every psychotherapy, even of the analytic kind, defines differently (even if often tacitly) what, according to its own criteria, is "a success". No one can adopt an objective external, meta-therapeutic attitude without taking into account what each theory and practice considers healing or improvement.

There's a well-known joke about a man who goes into analysis because he suffers from enuresis. After ten years he meets a friend and sings the praises of the analysis, which he is continuing. When his friend eventually asks impatiently: "So, do you still wet yourself or don't you?", the other replies: "Of course I still wet myself. But now I'm proud of it!" If, for a particular psychoanalytic current, it doesn't matter whether the symptom is dissolved, but what counts is that the subject can live with it, to the point of being proud of it, we have to consider this result a success from their point of view.

To this we should add that each psychotherapeutic theory has its own view of what is "mutative" in their practice. A cognitivist therapist may think that a patient has improved because of certain specific prescriptions with which they have complied, whereas a psychoanalytic reconstruction of the same therapy may see transference at play or the lifting of repressions and so on. One psychotherapy differs from another not only because it uses completely different intervention techniques but above all because it has a completely different view of what in medicine would be called the "active ingredient" of a therapy. A psychoanalyst may easily read a cognitivist treatment in terms of analytical dynamics, for example.[2]

In the absence of a clear answer to the question "which analytical technique is most effective?", I believe that most currents today lay claim to their own perspicuity. "Perspicuous" is an ambiguous concept. The sense of the word oscillates between something clear and manifest and something certain and obvious. Each school presents itself as more perspicuous than the others. Not as "the truest", since the concept of truth, if taken as scientific truth, today refers to protocols of verification and corroboration that are problematic in what I would call, rather than psychotherapies, logotherapies. Perspicuity therefore remains a subjective option, since what may be obvious and clear to me may not be so to you, and vice versa.

Perspicuity is connected to each analyst's general view of being human, a philosophical one in the broadest sense. Lacanians find Lacan's theories more perspicuous than those of other analysts because they share the Lacanian conception of what it means *to know*. But I would argue that we find more perspicuous what amuses us most intellectually.

Years ago, in America, I attended a clinical discussion conducted by a Lacanian analyst. Discussing a particular case, one participant objected that in addition to the Lacanian interpretation, it was possible to see it in terms of Kohut's theory, and he tried to develop an interpretation in that sense. To which the Lacanian analyst said: "Of course we can also see the case in Kohutian terms. But how very dull!" An approach other than our own, in short, bores us: it makes us yawn.

It's like philosophical choices: it would be extremely naive to claim that we embrace a certain philosophical approach because we find its logical arguments the most convincing. We embrace it because it comes across as more intellectually stimulating, interesting, alive. The arguments strengthen our initial sympathy for that theory. The concept of perspicuity is basically inseparable from that of intellectual enjoyment. Lacanians will find more pleasure when plunged into Lacanian theory, which sees in every psychic form a form of jouissance. I myself often prefer Lacanian concepts to those of other schools, precisely because Lacanian concepts lay bare something that gives me enjoyment. The elaboration of theories – even when these focus on pleasure – is itself a form of pleasure, even if for many the pleasure of theories can become a dangerous addiction, which can also lead to a certain blindness. Perhaps this is where the essential difference lies: it is one thing to derive pleasure from a theory, quite another to become addicted to it.

But as we can see, Lacanian theory gives me more enjoyment than others (in truth, not always) precisely because it starts from an assumption that is also my own: that a good part of our beliefs and intellectual travails are strategies for enjoyment (under which I also include the enjoyment of one's own power). A theory that unearths enjoyment everywhere is for me more pleasurable and plausible than a theory that everywhere sees survival functions, for example. But then, what relationship is there between enjoyment and truth? We all feel that theories and beliefs which please us are not necessarily true – false consciousness, Marxists would say. Here, I believe, lies the really big problem of any speculative philosophy.

What then separates a Lacanian from an ego-psychologist? As I've attempted to argue, it is not so much a clinical technique as a different view of subjectivity and ethics of our being-in-the-world. A Lacanian essentially rejects the following: adaptationism, the desire to strengthen the ego, the ideal of ego autonomy, the maturational vocation of psychoanalysis.

Lacanian anti-adaptationism arose as a reaction to an attempt by many analysts, not only American ones, to take up the notions of neo-Darwinism and introduce them to psychoanalysis. In fact, what counts in the evolutionary sciences is the fitness of organisms, their ability to adapt to the environment in which they live. In evolutionary science adaptation means the ability of a phenotype (organism) to reproduce its genotype: the greater its ability to do so, the better adapted it is. Transplanted into psychoanalysis, this fundamental principle of modern Neo-Darwinism leads to a fundamental ethical choice: that essentially the aim of analytical treatment is not, for example, to make individuals happier but to adapt them to their environment, and above all to their social one. This optimization of adaptation is achieved by strengthening the Ego of the second topic. So, Freud's famous prescription, *so es war, soll ich werden, (GW,* 15, p. 86) is translated and interpreted as: "where id was, there ego shall be".[3] Of course, they think that the id is neither removable nor completely controllable, just as the superego is neither removable nor controllable: we are constantly at the mercy of our drives (the Id) and a set of more or less strict moral demands (the Super-Ego). Moreover, we have to deal with the demands by our environment, especially those imposed by our fellow human beings, which require us to submit to common rules. The Ego is strengthened by channelling anti-social drives and freeing it from the burden of overly taxing moral prescriptions.

Now, this adaptive conception is very often criticized "from the left"; it is seen as a surrender to the demands of contemporary, that is, capitalist, society. Put simply: analysis serves to adapt us to our capitalist society. The adaptationist approaches to psychoanalysis are said to represent the psychoanalytic "right". However, this contrasts with the fact that there have always been many ego-psychology analysts who situate themselves on the political left, even the radical left. But though a strong left-wing Lacanian current has emerged in years, we cannot consider Lacanianism a "left-wing" version of psychoanalysis as opposed to a "right-wing" one, although in many cultural areas this very embodiment is being acted out. In any case, you would be hard pressed to find someone farther removed from the Lacanian left than myself.

For example, Cornelius Castoriadis – a French psychoanalyst known as a radical left-wing essayist – was strongly anti-Lacanian. But he criticized the American analytical currents and mocked the idea of certain *gringo* analysts who understood unemployment as a psychopathological symptom. "This is an aberration – he said – as well as idiotic, since unemployment is clearly an economy-related phenomenon" (Castoriadis and Benvenuto, 1998).

Take the case of unemployment, indeed. In Italy, many analysands bring the fact that they cannot find work as their symptom. This makes them dependent on their parents, spouses or others or on Italian welfare (the state provides the jobless with a minimal sum). These subjects complain of this lack of economic independence as an aspect of their persistent dependence on "nourishing" figures. Should I reply to these analysands as Castoriadis would have wanted and remove their sense of guilt, saying that the difficulty in finding work is just an objective economic problem in Italy today? But the fact that a lack of jobs is an objective problem does not prevent it from *also* being a subjective problem. Saying that they are merely victims of an economic situation would be by no means honest, because I very often find myself agreeing with them: there is something subjective preventing them from finding a serious job. Something "demonic" causes them to be fired soon after finding one; they fail to seize certain opportunities that are offered to them, they associate with people from whom clearly nothing concrete will ever materialize, they insist they want *a specific job* and refuse anything that minimally deviates from it. . . . They make no mistake in describing their inability to be economically independent as something ego-dystonic: "I like to work, but cannot . . ." Usually, at the heart of it all there's a need for a dependency that psychoanalysis calls oral; state welfare is a substitute for this oral dependency. All this – dynamics all analysts are familiar with – seems to go in the direction of the typical right-wing critique of the welfare state as a mechanism that infantilizes those who resort to it, one by which the state replaces a figure of a mother to depend on.

So, considering the subjective side of unemployment, is psychoanalysis an objectively conservative, right-wing practice? This is what the anti-psychoanalytic left – always very active among the Western intelligentsia – claims: psychoanalysis is a technique to integrate individuals into a neo-liberal logic.[4]

Personally, I believe that giving a left-wing and revolutionary sense to psychoa-nalysis, or giving it a conservative and right-wing sense, are two ways of not under-standing what analysis, which is neither left-wing nor right-wing, does.

It is a cliché to say that psychoanalysts merely treat YARVIS (young, articu-late, rich, verbal, intelligent, sophisticated) patients, while analysts actually help many to emerge from a fate of misery. Because neurotic inhibition produces mis-ery, it is just as true that a culture of poverty very often breeds certain kinds of neurosis. The two loops of economic poverty and neurosis are intertwined to the point that it is difficult to distinguish them and to say to what extent one causes the other.

An analyst never knows what *ultimately* precipitates a symptom. Does the sub-ject not find a job because of the high local unemployment rates? Is it because the subject indulges in an infantile position of being cared for by parental figures? Is it because the subject doesn't know how to step into the mental discipline of a working person? Is it because working also mostly means submitting to hierar-chically superior figures, something intolerable for the subject's narcissism? All these are factors, and they mix and boil together in the cauldron of distress, and the analyst has no means of untangling the various factors, despite Castoriadis's self-assuredness.

Yet analysts, even Lacanian ones, start from an ethical and technical assumption that is at once precise and bold: the *co-responsibility of subjects in their own fate*, including one of poverty. This assumption denounces what Lacan called – borrow-ing the concept from Hegel – *the beautiful soul*. A figure, I should say, dominant in our age of generalized rage against *Them* (those who hold large chunks of power). The beautiful souls, according to Lacan, are those who protest against the mess of the world in which they live as if they were not a part of it – "Only *They* are to blame" – without basically realizing how they, the beautiful souls themselves, contribute to the mess they condemn. So many rail against the state or the govern-ment, and then they evade taxes or hire people off the books or prefer to find an endorsement from "those in high places" to obtain a position rather than compete fairly with other candidates. . . . *Analysts do not believe in beautiful souls*, neither those of the left or those of the right. If a person comes to them and says "I've been trying to find a job for two years now, but no one will hire me in this lousy system!", the very first thing any analyst will think is that there's something rotten not in Denmark but in the person himself.

A Lacanian analyst would go even further and sometimes said that the analyst has to relate to the subject everything that happens to him or her: "If you've been diagnosed with cancer, well, you're responsible! In a way, it's you who wanted the cancer!" This seems to me a twisted point of view, which Susan Sontag (1978) rightly criticized in a well-known essay. But it shows how, even among Lacanians, the basic position of the analyst is the following: to see a subject's connivance with his or her own bitter fate, an assumption that many, and not always wrongly, deprecate. Because the analyst, from the illusion of beautiful souls, risks falling into an opposite delusion, that of ugly souls, of souls *always responsible* for their misfortunes. Here lies what I would call the analyst's interpretive tact: to realize to what extent they can show a subject how complicit they are with the demon that haunts them.

The ego psychologists' adaptationist recipe was then an easy, I would say approximate, way of describing the analyst's position. But what's the Lacanian position exactly?

Now, something that is quite striking is the absence in Lacan of any theory providing criteria for the progress of analysis (except perhaps in the very last phase of his teaching, but only in a very abstract and formal way). From time to time he would come up with an impressive statement on the subject, but there is no systematic theory on analytical healing. If we quote his statement that "analysis leads to a rectification of the subject's relationship to the real" (*E II*, 75), we could well give it an adaptational sense. But, as we've seen earlier in this text, Lacan was referring to an initial manoeuvre by analysis aimed at establishing transference with the analyst.

Still, if analysis rectifies the relationship with the real, what would then be the *right* relationship? Lacan doesn't say. No less because this rectification is absolutely subjective, there are no general criteria.

It could be argued that Lacan doesn't have a theory of healing through analysis because he doesn't think analysis should aim at healing. This is the so-called lay analysis, from the German *Laien*, secular, a non-medical analysis, one with no claim to healing. As Lacan says, you can be cured by analysis as a surplus. You undergo analysis for analysis's sake. But Lacan himself admits that the disappearance of symptoms – healing, to put it in a not very secular way – is the symptom, I dare say, that an analysis has been successful. No Lacanian would recognize as achieved an analysis where the subject still complains of disabling symptoms or takes up drugs or terrorist activities. . . . For a Lacanian, as for any analyst, there are indicators, so to speak, that an analysis has been successful. But they have never been theorized; they remain in the mists of presupposition.

Invoking the later Lacan, some argue that subjects need to find their *sinthome*, a neologism spelled differently from *symptôme*, symptom. We will not delve into the *sinthome* theory here. Suffice it to specify that *sinthome* does not coincide with the symptom, that is, with what the analysand complains of and would like to be relieved of. In any case, Lacan also foresees the end of symptoms (*symptômes*) as an analytic ideal.

In the 1970s Lacan came to Milan to meet his Italian followers, and I was among them. A young man asked him with deliberate naivety: "So, in the process of analysis that you describe, is there room for an elimination of symptoms?" Lacan replied that it was something self-evident. . . . He added, "even though we humans are very good at denying evidence". Lacan too believed that *obviously* analysis should heal.

In the same meeting Lacan said that he saw the effect of analysis as a *rapiéçage*, a patching up. He evoked a then-fashionable trait: wearing jackets with fake patches over the elbows. These additions can be beautiful, elegant, but they point to a rip, to a split seam, to something that, in short, even analysis cannot mend.

He was probably referring to the *sinthome* as patching up a fundamental rip in our subjectivity.

Very often, however, I notice a kind of double discourse in many Lacanians. On the one hand is the official discourse, which rejects any medical ideal of healing, of adaptation to the social context, of empowerment of the ego, of social success as a criterion. . . . On the other, when dealing with clinical cases, they implicitly apply an assessment of this very kind. There is a kind of intellectual hypocrisy.

During a clinical audit, a Lacanian analyst complained that a symptom of her analysand, in the analyst's view, was her failure to pass an important university exam. The implicit criterion is that if someone is analysed properly, they will pass exams. But is this not then the criterion of adaptation? And if the analysand stops smoking, for example, without any suffering, is this not a success of the analysis, in the sense of making someone overcome an addiction? But is not quitting an addiction itself an adaptation? It is as if in practice, even of the Lacanian kind, there was a manifest discourse – common to other "left-wing" variants of psychoanalysis – and a latent one, namely analysis as mental hygiene for individuals. And I wonder whether this inconsistency could somehow be a symptom of the theory, signalling its splitting.

Notes

1 Among the comparative studies on the effectiveness of psychotherapies, the most prominent are those by Luborsky and Singer (1975).
2 See Porcelli, 2004.
3 *SE*, 22, p. 79. But Freud writes "es", not "das Es"; he writes "ich", not "das Ich".
4 *Neo-liberale* in Italian, *néo-libéral* in French. The ambiguity of the word "liberal" in many languages is an important tool for mixing free market theory with "liberal" in the sense of civil rights movements, moderate left and so on. This confusion is at the core of the present fashion of the *pensée anti-libérale*.

Chapter 25

Analytic Idealities

As we know, for Lacan the project of strengthening the Ego – at the expense of the Id and the Super-Ego – is not authentically Freudian. In fact, it is precisely the Ego that represses, thus creating inhibitions and symptoms. Wanting to strengthen the Ego amounts to strengthening repressions. For Lacan, the Ego should not expand to the detriment of the Id (not of the unconscious, because according to Freud much of the Ego is unconscious too), but *I* have to install myself, as it were, in the Id. It is in this key that we should interpret Lacan's translation of Freud's *wo es war, soll ich werden*: "*Là où c'était, je dois advenir*".[1] Here the "*c*" is the contraction of *ça*, the French *es*. We could translate Lacan's translation as: "Where it was, there I have to become" (I translate the German *es* as "it"). As we can see, this is the opposite of the ego-psychological interpretation: "I" (in particular, and not "the ego") must constitute myself in the unconscious; I must "inhabit" it, not to say "colonize" it. It is not the ego that divests the unconscious, but I reach the unconscious and settle inside it.

Lacan's is evidently a Dionysian interpretation of Freud's thought and of analytic technique. I say "Dionysian" in the Nietzschean sense, even though Lacan does not explicitly refer to Nietzsche, nor to Georges Bataille. By Dionysian I mean a vision of the unconscious I called anti-military. The unconscious is not the barbarians from whom we need to defend ourselves, but it is a barbarism with which we need to live, from which to draw lifeblood and inspiration. The road has already been opened wide to the unconscious as the "desiring machines" of Deleuze and Guattari (1972).

Questions of technique in psychoanalysis are therefore inseparable from ethical directions, that is, the ideals that inspire an analyst's tactics and strategies. Now, Lacan himself, at the beginning of the seminar "The Ethics of Psychoanalysis", dwelt on what he considered the three fundamental ideals of every analyst: human love, authenticity and non-dependence (Se7, 17–20).

The ideal of human love often takes on among analysts the form of a celebration of genitality: the analysed man and woman – they claim – find fulfilment in monogamous love with one person (who could be someone of the same sex, as the most up-to-date analysts are ready to admit). This idealization of sexualized love, where sensuality and tenderness, sex and love, converge, certainly questions us

DOI: 10.4324/9781003388098-25

as to what then should be considered fulfilled, for example, in a child, who does not genitalize. In any case, Lacan sees a limit to this ideality in the fact that psychoanalysis has not investigated what he calls an *erotica*. This erotica is mapped by the ideal of human love but is not thematized by psychoanalysis. Here Lacan reproaches psychoanalysis for not being sufficiently creative.

As for the ideal of authenticity, this has taken different forms in various authors – in Winnicott (1960), for example, the liberation of the "true self" against the "false self". After all, we can all recognize an inauthentic person soon enough; we understand that they are always wearing a mask and that their falseness discredits them in the eyes of others, beginning with the members of their own family – even if they often fail to understand the reason for this discredit. Consider all those young insecure intellectuals, afraid of being judged, flaunting their under-digested culture by "talking like textbooks". Let us give credit to the unmasked, to those who don't disguise themselves behind socially acceptable behaviour. Lacan stresses that this ideality does not coincide with that of many classical philosophies and traditional moral discourses, that of a *practice of virtues*. Or rather, psychoanalysis tacitly admits that the practice of the ideal of authenticity also entails a more virtuous subjectivity, but the virtuous woman and man are not the explicit ideal end of analysis. An increase in virtue comes, in short, in the same way as healing in analysis, as a surplus, as something that the analyst does not pursue and happens nonetheless. It is as if the analyst were saying: "First of all be authentic. (Then, perhaps, you will also be more virtuous)".

We see here the analogy between Lacanian analysis and the techniques of Zen Buddhism,[2] in that the latter do not aim at wisdom or virtue but at *satori*, a state of enjoyment of which Western culture has no concept.

I would then place as a corollary of this ideality the commitment to absolute sincerity. It is not acceptable for an analyst to lie to an analysand, not even for their own good, to spare them pain, for example. The analyst may refrain from speaking certain truths but cannot speak untruths, because the analyst's sincerity – which should be a model for the analysand's – is the way the ideal of authenticity unfolds. But of course, the duty of sincerity goes beyond the professional ethics of the analyst: it reverberates with an ideal of sincerity that is a fundamental trait of our modern culture. Even if our social relations are as hypocritical as they have almost always been, we experience a sense of guilt, a malaise, in our social life that clashes with the ideal of authenticity. Significantly, in the United States in particular, a politician can be forgiven anything except one thing: lying. Also in America, an ethic prevails that obliges the members of a couple to be always absolutely truthful, even if it means revealing extremely embarrassing thoughts and desires.

As for the ideal of non-dependence (analysis as preventive care against dependence), here too Lacan differentiates it from a more traditional ideality, that of an educational orthopaedics aimed at establishing healthy habits in subjects or giving them "a strong personality".

Instead, psychoanalysis rather aims at dissolving all forms of dependence. First, I would say, to the parents but also to surrogate addictions: drugs, alcohol, gambling, even sex. . . . (Some, in my opinion, have a problem of addiction to Lacan, off which they should be weaned). We notice, however, that the ideal of a greater autonomy of the ego, on which ego psychology insists, is nothing other than the other face of the ideal of non-dependence or more independence. Here Lacan seems to share the ideality of his opponents.

As for me, I would distinguish between the ideal of non-dependence and the ideal of wisdom. Analytical practice does not claim, for instance, to be a conscience check that ought to lead to a Stoic subjectivity (conscience checks were a typical practice of Stoic philosophers). But just as erotica and virtue are something analysis plus-produces – in the sense that it produces them as a surplus, without their being its target – similarly we expect analysed subjects to gain access to a certain wisdom, something the analysts do not preach but, if they're lucky, practise.

I would add something that derives from my own practice, something ultimately in line with Freud's original intuition: that if we scrape the barrel of people's psychic problems, we always find a non-separation from the figures, wills, desires and ways of being of someone's childhood. A subject suffers because of wanting, on the one hand, to live as an independent woman or man, who knows what she or he wants, while, on the other, still being completely entangled in infantile ways of being. Sooner or later, and sooner rather than later, what appears in adults undergoing analysis is the child they have ultimately continued to be, something Lacan described with the aphorism "the unconscious is the discourse of the Other", read: of the adult. It is therefore not only a question of dependence but of the unthinkability of being different from what we originally were, infants completely trapped in the world of the adults who take care of us or neglect us.

We can ask ourselves, however, to what extent Lacan accepts these idealities as constitutive of any analytic activity, of whichever school or trend, or whether he is not sketching here a sort of tacit critique of these idealities. Significantly, he speaks of "ideologies" with regard to these idealities – and ideology, in Marxist terminology, is false consciousness (but Lacan was not a Marxist). Everything would suggest, however, that Lacan also takes up these ideologies in his own practice, but it is as if he did so unwillingly. And it is interesting to note how he fails to develop any sort of conceptualization of them: all the subsequent seminars of that year completely neglected the analyst's idealities but dealt with the essential ethical dimension in human life. It's as if Lacan were somewhat ashamed to summarize these idealities, which seem to be not only the essential source of analytic work but also one of the limits of psychoanalysis. In any case, as we have seen, there is no space for the reinforcement of the ego. But what if by reinforcement of the Ego, his opponents meant precisely that which results from the three idealities or ideologies shared by Lacan?

In any case, it would be naïve to insist on the neutrality of the analyst, on the a-morality of analysis, on analysis as a purely non-evaluative practice, reducible to mere technique. Instead, analytic idealities decisively steer the entire practice, "the technique", of analysis. And I would say that these ideals are also the basis of a certain prestige that psychoanalysis still enjoys – despite all the attacks and mockery – in the so-called Western world. The analyst enjoys a certain authority, even in the eyes of analysands, because he champions these idealities – human love, authenticity, non-dependence – which are also, in fact, the idealities of our age. That is, of the elites of our age (after all, the image we receive of every age is given to us by its elites). Because on the one hand we have what Lacan calls "capitalist discourse" – that is, the utilitarian calculation of the *do ut des*, the competitive form of life – but on the other we also have psychoanalytic discourse, which is an expression of an ethics that permeates democratic-liberal (capitalist) societies themselves and which at once integrates and corrects these societies. Perhaps this ethics is the discourse of a cosmopolitan and metropolitan elite but nevertheless of a ruling elite.

The accusation often thrown at psychoanalysis – of being an elitist practice for wealthy YARVIS subjects – is also a way of obliquely recognizing in it a certain social excellence as the practice of an ideality that belongs to a prestigious class, in the sense that it rules the moral evolution of our society, and is being opposed today by a certain populist and neo-fascist backlash. Here we take "ruling elites" to mean not only the wealthiest – because even today we continue to view the economy as the key to social life – but also those we generally refer to today as *influencers*, who wield a cultural influence on others.

(By ruling elite, therefore, I mean not only the major bankers, entrepreneurs and politicians but anybody who is considered socially successful: admired university professors, popular artists, writers and journalists, big media managers, high level clergymen, top magistrates, senior bureaucrats. . . . This elite also includes, of course, anti-capitalist and leftist theoreticians, insofar as they are socially success-ful. These elites provide psychoanalysts with the vast majority of their clients.)

As is clear, my analysis overturns a conception that was mainstream in the last century: that there is something subversive, anti-capitalist and revolutionary about psychoanalysis. Instead, I believe that psychoanalysis is an organic part of liberal-democratic societies just as the field hospital is an organic part of a warring army. Psychoanalysis is an eminent expression of our *Kultur*, in the same way as, to make one comparison, the flourishing of mendicant orders like the Franciscans in the late Middle Ages not only expressed a reaction to the temporal power of the church of the time but above all represented a spiritual need of the time.

So, when we look at these ideals summarized by Lacan more closely, we realize that ego psychology has merely said the same things, albeit in language which is by no means philosophically correct. The ideal of human love becomes the idealiza-tion of the genital relationship and the adaptation, so to speak, of every person to her or his partner. The ideal of authenticity is reformulated as a reinforcement of the ego, insofar as only a strong ego, that is, a flexible one, can sustain an authentic-ity that doesn't amount to a pure surrender to the dynamics of the drives or submis-sion to a super-egoic prescriptiveness. The ideal of non-dependence is summed up in the ideal of the independent, mature Ego: that is, a subject separated from the mother (from the Other, Lacan would say) and individualized.

Notes

1 *E 1*, 414, 521. *E 2*, 2, 62, 281, 322, 344–345.
2 See Charraud (2011).

Chapter 26

A Non-Psychological Psychoanalysis

Lacan is said to be in conflict with ego psychology insofar as it formulates an attempt – which will also be practised by other psychoanalytic currents – to reconcile psychoanalysis and general psychology.

General psychology at that time was concerned with memory, logical and calculating abilities; the representation of the world of subjects; and so on – in short, with what we today call cognitive faculties. Ego psychologists wanted to show that the Freudian conception of the unconscious could be a pillar of the cognitive sciences (as we would call them today) as a whole. Hence the idea of a desexualized area of the ego. Indeed, in our daily lives we are not always plunged in the unconscious: we work, we rationalize, we keep informed, make calculations, compete, plan things. . . . All of this "emerged" part of the psyche needed to be seized back by psychoanalysis through the notion of the Ego of the second topic, as the organizer of the normal, conscious functions of the psyche, as the *executive power* (the government) of the psyche, to stay in line with our political metaphor. The notion of Ego served as a bridge between psychoanalysis as a theory and practice of the unconscious and psychology as the study of the mind.

Lacan, on the contrary, began from a completely different vision. His relationship to general psychology is somewhat similar to the relationship that Marxism, especially after Marx, had and still has with modern political economics. Marxist economics is certainly a very specific economic theory – referred to as "classical" because it is based on the classical economic thought of Smith and Ricardo – but it is also a "critique of economics", an anti-economics. Marxism is not only a theory that explains the establishment of economic value but also a deconstruction of how value is established. Marxism has therefore gradually detached itself from economic knowledge as it has been established over the last two centuries: it is a sort of shadow of economic thought, a philosophical view in the broad sense of economic efficiency as such.

In somewhat the same way, Lacan saw psychoanalysis as an anti-psychology, an implicit *critique of psychology*. Lacan would say that psychoanalysis is not a branch of psychology but something heterogeneous to it – an *erotology*. It seeks to be not only a discipline of the unconscious as such, one that puts all other psychic functions in brackets, but a theory of the origin of the psychic as such. Unlike any

DOI: 10.4324/9781003388098-26

descriptive psychology, for Lacan psychoanalysis starts from what we can call the *arché* – the inception, the beginning, the rule – of psychic life, that which governs it: desire and enjoyment. *Die Lust*, as Freud called it. Unlike psychology, psychoanalysis focuses on a constitutive essence of the psychic, which Freud at one point called Eros and Thanatos.

What seems evident is Lacan's indifference to – rather than rejection of – the psychology of his time (evolutionary or experimental) and of some of the other human sciences, such as certain forms of sociology or political economy. But Lacan also gave great importance to other types of human sciences. Lacan highly valued structural linguistics (especially Jakobson) and a part of cultural anthropology (Lévi-Strauss), not to mention logic and certain branches of mathematics. In fact, Lacan did not despise psychology or sociology as such but rather *certain* psychological and sociological theories that were popular at the time. Non-structural theories made him shrug.[1]

If, therefore, a structural psychology or sociology had developed at the time, Lacan would certainly have taken an interest. After all, he attached great importance to mathematical game theory – without imagining that this theory would become one of the pillars of cognitive science, of a way of thinking far removed from psychoanalysis. He was also interested in the thought of Gregory Bateson,[2] that is, the theory of biological systems and the ecology of the mind, which would later be adopted as the basis of systemic family psychotherapies in many European countries. I am convinced he would have very much appreciated the sociological thought of Niklas Luhmann, for example, had he been acquainted with it; thus, sociology too would have entered the ranks of the human sciences "that don't dilly-dally".[3] And he would probably have been attracted to the approaches of certain neuroscientists, for example, that of Gerald Edelman (1987, 1991).

What do all these theories – post-Saussurian linguistics, structural anthropology, mathematical logic, topology, game theory – have in common for him to consider them so important? The answer is the structural approach. Many deny that Lacan can be inscribed within so-called French structuralism, which the Americans later called post-structuralism. But there is no doubt that Lacan was attracted to theories based on systemic and formal descriptions, mostly based on a priori paradigms. Saussure's systemic approach to languages seemed to him exemplary of a rigorous approach, and not only to language. In other words, what matters are the relations not between full entities but between differential, purely distinctive ones. In short, Lacan appreciated the sciences that found in their object the fundamental structure of language. Today we would say – imbued as we are with information technology – that Lacan gave absolute priority to the digital over the analogical. He was only interested in theories that digitized their object. So, even what an old tradition considered extra-linguistic, animal, in human beings – emotions, instincts, imprinting, affections, empathy and so on – should be seen from a digital point of view, that is, as steeped in language.

On the other hand, Lacan was unconcerned with anything that aimed at quantification (even through experimental protocols), at increasingly accurate measurements.

Above all, he loathed anything "evolutionary", any theories or studies that aimed at showing how to achieve the best: how a child becomes an adult, how a primitive human becomes civilized, how the magical becomes scientific, how the religious becomes purely ethical and so on. He did not believe in describing a development towards a supposed optimum, which is always what a researcher has reached or claims to have reached. For this reason, he was not very keen on the theories of Jean Piaget, insofar as they were descriptions of a child's journey, stage after stage, towards a particular supposed adult accomplishment.

In general, Lacan was fond of *a priori* sciences and rejected *a posteriori* ones. A certain Cartesian rationalism certainly acted in him, an exaltation of the *mos geometricus* and a parallel rejection of the empirical, calculative, inferential or – to use C.S. Peirce's expression – abductive sciences.[4] He preferred deduction starting from abstract formal systems. These options oriented not only Lacan's scientific preferences but also those of more than one generation of Parisian *intellectuels*.

To aim for structures is to find something like the game of chess in human life (Saussure himself referred to chess as a metaphor for linguistic structure).[5] As in chess, each variation involves a restructuring of the entire field of relationships. He aimed at describing the psyche as a set of mathematical relations. But this *esprit de géométrie* is continually combined in Lacan – and this gave him great success – with two other sensibilities: one is the fundamental Freudian concept of the primacy of the drive and the libidinal; the other is a vision that I would call existentialist. I believe that the remarkable charm Lacanian thought wields on many is the effect of the way it puts together in a non-coarse way three anthropologies that appear very different from each other: a structuralist anthropology, a Freudian one of the primacy of *Lust* understood in a Dionysian key and an existentialist one based on a primal loss of being by humans, on human beings as "useless passion", as Sartre would have put it.

By existentialism I mean wanting to see a fundamental flaw or incompleteness in the human being, which Lacan attributes to the access to language humans have. Along these lines, so-called psychopathology would seem to be the very model of "normal" human existence: there is something deficient in the very essence of the human being. That is, the human being's relationship to everything instinctual – sexuality, food, moods – is by its very structure somehow always disturbed. For Lacan, the implantation of language into humans has caused in them a fundamental *désêtre* (dis-being), a lack of being that is the basis of human *détresse* (distress). No less than Freud, Lacan is a pessimistic thinker. And it is precisely this pessimism that makes him popular, insofar as scepticism, pessimism, and disenchantment appear in our post-Christian culture as the mark of superior men and women, those not mixed with the masses. And superior women and men are those who *do not delude themselves*. They do not delude themselves, for example, that there can finally be a happy society, a permanent state of satisfaction. Thanks to Lacan, however, these typical characteristics of superior women and men appear instead as defining characteristics of any human being, even the humblest. Lacanianism is in its own way a modernist ennobling of human beings.

Thus, Lacan has knotted together three demands that many see as opposites, as incompatible: on the one hand, the fascination with structural reconstructions in geometrical order; on the other, a kind of ontological pessimism, the conviction that there is something rotten in human essence, insofar as at once produced and contaminated by language; and on the other, a conative vision of the human essence, human life as shaped by *jouissance*.

So, even in clinical practice Lacan preferred a structural approach. That is, he was not interested in describing psychic *processes*: he was interested in formal relations. This is one reason I do not believe that his brief flirtation with Kleinian practice, which consists entirely in the handling of processes, was entirely sincere. Lacan, even in his clinical approach, was interested in a set of differences and oppositions. Not in an evolution in a certain direction, but in "leaps" from one position to another. *Anima facit saltus.*

All this explains his interest in Professor Brain. It was a case that seemed emblematic of the dizzying nature of the concept of the Other that he was developing. Because Professor Brain can grasp what is intimate in his mind, *his own* ideas, only thanks to an imaginary alienation whereby *his own* appears as a theft inflicted *on the Other*. The Other is therefore not someone or another but a place of non-property, of in-appropriateness; it is a formal and non-substantial Other. But on the other hand, at the level of enunciation – that is, of a confrontation between rivals over the Freudian inheritance – Lacan operates something that is the opposite of our imaginary plagiarist: he struggles to recognize the fact that, just as there is no plagiarism, there is also no *legitimate analysis*, as opposed to one that would be illegitimate. Lacan seems to lack the necessary alienation underlying all allegiance: precisely insofar as you are inspired by Freud, by the Master, you betray him. There is a kind of compulsion to be unfaithful, which is the opposite of plagiarism. Just as we always steal our ideas from the Other, conversely we always betray the ideas of the others by appropriating them and thus ipso facto alienating them. Our appropriation of the Other always results in a modification of the Other's property: through theft, we transform what we steal. In this sense, Lacan's syndrome seems to be the inverse of Professor Brain's: it claims a fidelity (to Freud) where there can only be an infidelity, an infidelity intrinsic to all appropriation.

In fact, we could apply Lacan's theory of object *a*, described as the "cause of desire", to Lacan himself. At the source of desire, therefore, there is not only the drive but also an inaugural object that causes us. The point is that with Lacan we always try to find this causative object, but what we find is *always another object*, an ersatz, a surrogate, and as such always disappointing. We try to recover something initial, but in the meantime we deviate and find a substitute. The desire to return to Freud also obeys the same detachment. After all, Freud is Lacan's object *a*; Freud causes his thought, but what he finds in the end is something other than Freud, something Lacanian, very Lacanian.

In this way the two inverted syndromes – the imaginary plagiarism and the myth of a Return to Freud – shed light on the analytic process itself. Lacan uses Kris's case to raise questions about analytical technique. In fact, *who interprets* in analysis? Lacan's answer is that the analysand analyses while the analyst interprets. But Lacan himself makes it possible for the interpretation too to come from the analysand. The best interpretation is the one that comes from the analysand. So here too we have an alienation: analysands can only access their own interpretations by somehow stealing them from their Other, from the analyst. But the analysts themselves can recognize a good interpretation insofar as it comes from their own Other, that is, from psychoanalytic doctrine, which they have established as the guarantor of truth, that is, as their own Other.

It is here that analysis risks entering a maze where the position of the Other prepares to alienate itself continually: either the analysand's subjectivity is reduced to a simple scholastic dependence on the analyst's mindset (the Other as analyst is reduced to the analyst's language, or rather jargon), or the analyst allows her to be carried away, like a raft in the ocean, by the analysand's associations. Analysis then seems to proceed on this tightrope between two abysses: either that of a disguised didactic, as the transplantation into the analysand's mind of a school-based way of interpreting, or that of analysis as *dérive*, a term which in French means both *to derive* and *drift*. The analyst goes adrift for years behind the analysand's fluctuations.

Notes

1 See Zafiropoulos (2001).
2 At his seminar, back in 1958 – when Bateson was still completely unknown in France – Lacan had Gisela Pankow comment on the Batesonian theory of the *double bind*: see *Se5*, ch. VIII, pp. 143–147. See also *Se20*, ch. XI. See Bateson (1972, 1979) and G. Bateson and M.C. Bateson (1987).
3 *"Branlants dans le manche"*. An expression Lacan used in *Se7*, p. 373. See also: Benvenuto (2020), pp. 74–75.
4 On abduction according to C.S. Peirce, see Eco and Sebeok (1988).
5 See Swiggers (2014).

Chapter 27

Psychoanalytic Exhibit

With this work, which is now drawing to a close, I wanted to give an example of how we can analyse a theoretical and clinical psychoanalytic text using a method similar to that of psychoanalysis itself. I do not mean that it is necessary to psychoanalyse analysts, in the sense of bringing the fantasies their texts may "betray", in the various senses of *betray* (being a turncoat, being an unfaithful partner and unintentionally disclosing something), even though these personal phantasies can of course also emerge. With this case we have seen aspects of the man Lacan, of his more or less recognized ambitions, of his problems with writing, but that is not what is essential. So the term "psychoanalysing psychoanalysts" could steer us off course, and I would instead suggest the term *deconstructing*, already well established in philosophy and literary criticism.

We owe the fortune of this term to Derrida, who associates it with *analysis* insofar as the etymology of "analysis" is αναλυειν, to loosen. To deconstruct a text is to untie its knot. A philosophical text – but a psychoanalytical one too – ties lines of reasoning, but the knot must then be untied. In his own way, Derrida also attempted a "psychoanalysis" of philosophical and psychoanalytic texts, particularly of Freud and Lacan. Deconstructing a theoretical text certainly does not mean criticizing it, dismantling its arguments, revealing its groundlessness . . . far from it. In some ways, it is an act of devotion towards both the deconstructed texts and those who produced them.

We can also refer to a fundamental distinction in Wittgenstein's thought: that between *saying* and *showing*, which can also be taken as a philosophical reformulation of what I distinguished previously, statement and utterance.

According to Wittgenstein, philosophers cannot say everything; indeed, they must recognize that with regard to certain things – particularly ethical and aesthetical ones – *they can say nothing*. Yet the things that philosophers cannot say may – if they are rigorous in their logic – *reveal themselves* in what they write. For example, in his *Tractatus Logico-Philosophicus*, Wittgenstein only touches upon ethics briefly, but he wrote (in a letter to the publisher of the book)[1] that the unspoken meaning of that book was purely ethical. That is, for him, that book, actually a cast-iron concatenation of arguments, revealed something ethical that the book itself could not say.

DOI: 10.4324/9781003388098-27

The profound analogy between this distinction of Wittgenstein's and analytical work is evident: Analysts too focus on their analysands' *word*, on their saying (and words also include gestures, acts, *eloquent* behaviours), but they do so to make something that "betrays itself" – that unwittingly reveals itself but that also changes field – reappears through this word, and this is what they call the unconscious. But the point is: can the unconscious that emerges in analysis really be *said*? It certainly can, but then it's no longer analysis, it's explanation. . . . And in fact, only very naïve analysts would undertake to say verbally to their analysands that which *reveals itself* as their unconscious. If an analyst says it, the unconscious ceases to manifest itself. This is the paradox or, if you like, the limit, of analysis, which Lacan, in his own way, sought, even more than to say, to show. And he summed it up in the adage "that which one might be saying remains forgotten behind what is said in what is heard".[2] The act of saying remains forgotten, therefore, but can be shown, reshown I would say, through another saying.

This disconnection between theory and act in analysis can also be found in the analysis of psychoanalytic and philosophical texts itself. Here we can only briefly touch upon this possibility. Usually at school or university we are only taught philosophical statements (*énoncés*), what a philosopher *says*, as if that were the essential point. Of course, we need to understand what a philosopher said, but does understanding it amount to understanding only that? Something behind the philosophical saying can be reconstructed, that is, led to saying, since it shows itself through that saying. But saying what a philosopher shows . . . amounts to changing philosophy.

This is evident when we are drawn to a particular philosophical theory that appears to express something of our own thought. Can we honestly say that we prefer it, that we embrace it, because its arguments are superior to those of other philosophical theories, as is the case with mathematics? Certainly, philosophical reflection on mathematics is fundamental, but philosophy itself is not mathematics; that is, it is not *essentially* based on logical demonstrations. A philosophical theory of mathematics cannot be a meta-mathematics, just as a philosophical theory of language cannot be a meta-language. What makes us love or adopt a philosophy is not a logical consequence of its syllogisms but the fact that that that philosophy expresses something that philosophy itself cannot say and that is shown through it. And what shows itself in a philosophy is what wins us over, or conversely what repels us. By trying to *prove*, even rigorously, philosophy *shows*. We can say that logical argumentation is the rhetoric of philosophy: it is a way of persuading the reader of the validity of what one wants to show.

The point is that if we were able to say what that object *a* (as Lacan would say) that shows itself in a philosophy and sometimes seduces us is, we would already be elsewhere from that philosophy, because we would have "analysed" it, deconstructed it. To understand why we *really* prefer a philosophy is to relativize it, perhaps therefore not to prefer it anymore, in the same way as the analyst helps the subject to position himself elsewhere from the place where he was before analysis.

I wanted this text to be an example of what we can take to be a deconstructive reading of psychoanalytic texts, to reconstruct what shows itself in a psychoanalytic theory – to indicate its object *a* – is to deconstruct it, because that is the way to lay bare a need that does not show but inspires thought. We should ask ourselves: "By opting for this way of seeing things, what does this analyst want to *show*? Does he want to show his personal way of doing analysis? Or does he want to show an implicit metaphysics about the humans in which he believes? Or does he want to propose a certain ideal of analytic practice?" In our study of Lacan, this is what emerged: what was at stake in his return to Freud and in his bitter critique of ego psychology was symbolic, a posing as Freud's legitimate heir. But this symbolic stake unravelled as an imaginary struggle against "pope Kris". In fact, the pope is the legitimate heir to Saint Peter.

Today, the rules of the game have changed because, as we said, very few analysts still claim to be faithful to Freud's thought. On the contrary, they take credit for showing how much they innovate with respect to Freud, how fruitfully they move away from the original ideas! Lacan therefore won the match for lack of opponents: the Lacanians are practically the only ones who claim to be *truly Freudian*. The inheritance they claimed was merrily granted to them. But, here too, what is it that shows itself in Lacan's struggle to state the essential in Freud?

The point is that an inheritance is always a change of ownership: the property that belonged to someone who died is passed on to the heirs. In the case of a doctrine such as psychoanalysis, it is a change of ownership of the *sense* of the writings of the deceased. But Lacan himself told us that there is no private appropriation of ideas, and ultimately not even of letters. If Lacan was so interested in Kris's case, it is because it questions the relationship between writing and a subject, whether writer or reader, insofar as it is not a relationship of appropriation. There is a focal point in his work here, which took the form not only of teaching but also of writing. What *shows itself* here – in his insistence on Brain – of his certainly problematic relationship with what he called the instance of the letter?

Lacan's career began and ended by thematizing writing. In 1932, his dissertation on psychiatry attracted a great deal of interest, even among the literati, because Lacan had done something psychiatrists did not usually do. His paranoid patient, whom he calls Aimée in his dissertation, wrote poems, and, instead of scrapping them, putting them in the *poubelle*, he published them as part of the thesis. These poems were highly appreciated by the Surrealist poets; Dali quoted her in an essay in the magazine *Le Minotaure*, and Joe Bousquet republished some of Aimée's poems in his magazine *14, rue du Dragon*. From the very beginning, therefore, Lacan's interest in the unconscious was bound up with a special focus on psychotic writing. And when he devoted an entire seminar year to psychosis (*Seminar III*) in 1955–6, he significantly focused almost entirely on a written text, Schreber's *Memoirs of My Nervous Illness* (Schreber, 1903), a book for which he spared no praise even for its literary value. His interest in mad writing was the A and the Z of his work. (Some maliciously say that Lacan's writing itself has a psychotic mark.)

That Lacan always linked psychosis and writing is confirmed by what he recommends to analysts when confronted with psychotics: to be their secretaries or scribes.[3] Not in the sense that analysts should materially transcribe what psychotics say but in the sense that they should never interpret their words, but instead "transcribe" them, repeat them as if they were writing under dictation. As if they were noting down a witness's statements. Analysts need to transform the psychotic saying into letters.

But the point is that even before saying this, Lacan had already asserted (in 1953) that *in any analysis*, the analyst is a scribe: "Witness . . . , depositary . . . , reference . . . , guarantor . . . , custodian . . . , *tabellion* [a public servant with some of the functions of a notary] . . , the analyst has something of the scribe".[4] He often said that "the analyst writes"; his or her function is equated with someone who turns the subject's word into writing. It is a repetition of the word, as writing was in its beginnings. A writing, however, which in this case is immaterial.

The various writings that make up the *Écrits* are presented in strict chronological order, except one, the first: the seminar on Poe's *Purloined Letter*. That seminar seemed worthy of opening his *Writings* because it had to do with a misappropriated, stolen piece of writing, and here we find again the theme of plagiarism as a plundering of writings. And worthy of note is also the fact that his last truly significant seminar – *Le sinthome*, his 20th – addresses James Joyce and his writing. We can say that, ideally at least, Lacan's work opens with the *poubellication* (a pun between *poubelle*, "rubbish", and "publication") of Aimée's psychotic poems and concludes with a writing that Lacan considered psychotic, Joyce's. His written work also begins with an analysis of a written work (Poe's *The Purloined Letter*), which in turn concerns a letter. In fact, in psychosis we see a certain freedom of letters, which no longer seem to be guided by a subjective project: the letters impose themselves on the subject, who, as in inspired writings, only becomes their spokesperson. In other words, according to Lacan, analysts duplicate the psychotic position: they do not write their own material but *transcribe* what the other says.

Lacan put the signifier in the foreground, but by placing his interest in letters in a key position, he shows us something that goes beyond his saying. Lacan's very special relationship to the letter, to writing, is psychotic in style, since in psychosis letters act on the subject as real objects. But whatever issue Lacan was trying to unravel, through Aimée's poems, Poe's purloined letter, Brain's imaginary plagiarism, Schreber's written memoirs, Joyce's "nonsense" writing, . . . , Lacan speaks to any of us who pose the problem of the subject's, any subject's, relationship with language, which is never private, personal, an object of appropriation, posing the question of what is really *ours*.

Here we can only highlight this issue that shows itself. But just as Lacan's analysis of Joyce cannot itself be Joycean, so too an analysis of Lacan's text that finally succeeds in saying what it shows cannot be a Lacanian one.

In public meetings I'm sometimes asked: "What will be the future of Lacanian psychoanalysis?" I reply that the question should rather be: "What will be the future of psychoanalysis?"

Even beyond their considerable differences, the various psychoanalytic schools often fail to realize that they're in the same boat and face the same hurricanes. No analytic school is the solution to the crisis of psychoanalysis, which certainly exists in many countries. The internal civil war between analysts should give rise not to an alliance but to the elimination of all that is outdated, dead, in each of these schools. It is Freud's gamble that needs to be carried forward, not one of the ways in which it has been read, interpreted or modified.

When 20 years ago psychoanalysis went through a crisis in France – a country where for 40 years it had enjoyed an uninterrupted very high prestige – the crisis did not affect any school in particular but *all* psychoanalytic schools and institutions. Something somewhat like the crisis of the political left in recent decades in the West, in particular the fact that it has become the option of the upper-middle and more educated classes, while it has been abandoned by the more disadvantaged classes. This abandonment of the left by the "subordinate classes" has not affected the moderate left, the reformist left or the radical left selectively: it has actually affected every single component of the left. What has been abandoned is the emancipatory project of every type of left.

This book of mine, by re-establishing the conflicts between psychoanalytic trends in their proper dimension, wants to contribute in its own way to an awareness of a psychoanalytic challenge that goes beyond the legacies of the old conflicts towards which the younger generations can only feel alien.

Notes

1 In Janik (1996 [1979]).
2 In "L'Etourdi", *Aut. E.,* 449.
3 *Se 3*, 233. *Sem 3*, 244.
4 Lacan, "Fonction et champ de la parole et du langage", in *E*, p. 313.

References

Althusser, L. 2014, *Ideology and Ideological State Apparatuses*, Verso, London and New York.

Austin, J.L. 1962, *How to Do Things with Words: The William James Lectures Delivered at Harvard University in 1955*, Clarendon Press, Oxford.

Baños Orellana, J. 2002, *L'écritoire de Lacan*, EPEL, Paris.

Bartlett, F.C. 1932, *Remembering*, Cambridge University Press, Cambridge.

Bateson, G. 1972, *Steps to an Ecology of Mind*, Chandler Publishing Company, San Francisco.

Bateson, G. 1979, *Mind and Nature: A Necessary Unity*, Fontana, London.

Bateson, G. and Bateson, M.C. 1987, *Angels Fear: Towards an Epistemology of the Sacred*, Macmillan, New York.

Benveniste, E. 1966, 'De la subjectivité dans le langage', in *Problèmes de linguistique générale*, vol. I, Gallimard, Paris, pp. 258–266.

Benveniste, E. 1974, 'L'appareil formel de l'énonciation', in *Problèmes de linguistique générale*, vol. II, Gallimard, Paris, pp. 79–88.

Benvenuto, S. 2016, *What Are Perversions?* Karnac, London.

Benvenuto, S. 2019, 'Autism: A battle lost by psychoanalysis (autism and psychoanalysis)', *Division/Review. A Quarterly Psychoanalytic Forum*, 19, pp. 26–32.

Benvenuto, S. 2020, 'On autism. Response to my critics', *Division/Review. A Quarterly Psychoanalytic Forum*, 20, pp. 29–33.

Bettelheim, B. 2001, *Freud and Man's Soul*, Pimlico, London.

Borsche, T. 1981, *Sprachansichten: Der Begriff der menschlichen Rede in der Sprachphilosophie Wilhelm von Humboldts*, Klett-Cotta, Stuttgart.

Campo, A. 2020, 'Quel pasticciaccio del Professor Brain', *Fata Morgana* (15-XII-2020), www.fatamorganaweb.it/la-ballata-del-mangiatore-di-cervella/

Castoriadis, C. and Benvenuto, S. 1998, 'A conversation between Sergio Benvenuto and Cornelius Castoriadis', *Journal of European Psychoanalysis*, 6, www.journal-psychoanalysis.eu/articles/a-conversation-between-sergio-benvenuto-and-cornelius-castoriadis-1/

Charraud, N. 2011, 'Lacan et le bouddhisme chan', *La Cause freudienne*, 3(79), pp. 122–126.

Cosenza, D. 2023, *A Lacanian Reading of Anorexia*, Routledge, London.

de Duarte, A.L. 1997, 'Crónica de una distorsión en psicoanálisis', *Asociación Escuela Argentina de Psicoterapia para Graduados*, 17.

Deazley, R., Kretschmer, M. and Bently, L. eds. 2010, *Privilege and Property: Essays on the History of Copyright*, Open Book Publishers, Cambridge.

Deleuze, G. and Guattari, F. 1972 [2004], *Anti-Oedipus: Capitalism and Schizophrenia* (Eng. trans. by Robert Hurley, Mark Seem and Helen R. Lane), Continuum, London and New York (Vol. 1 of *Capitalism and Schizophrenia*. 2 vols., 1972–1980).

Eco, U. and Sebeok, T.A. 1988, *The Sign of Three: Dupin, Holmes, Peirce (Advances in Semiotics)*, Indiana University Press, Bloomington.

Edelman, G.M. 1987, *Neural Darwinism: The Theory of Neuronal Group Selection*, Basic Books, New York.

Edelman, G.M. 1991, *Bright Air, Brilliant Fire: On the Matter of Mind*, Basic Books, New York.

Ferenczi, S. 1928 [1955], 'The elasticity of psycho-analytic technique', in M. Balint ed. (1955), Final Contributions to the problems and Methods of Psychoanalysis vol. III. Basic Books, New York, pp. 87–102.

Festinger, L. 1957, *A Theory of Cognitive Dissonance*, Stanford University Press, Paolo Alto.

Fink, B. 2004, *Lacan to the Letter*, University of Minnesota Press, Minneapolis and London.

Freud, A. 1946, *The Ego and the Mechanisms of Defense* (trans. Cecil Baines), International Universities Press, New York.

Freud, S. 1905a, 'Jokes and their relation to the unconscious', *SE*, 8, pp. 1–236.

Freud, S. 1905b, 'Fragments of an analysis of a case of hysteria', *SE*, 7, pp. 1–122.

Freud, S. 1909a, 'Analysis of a phobia in a five-year-old boy (Little Hans)', *SE*, 10, pp. 5–148.

Freud, S. 1909b, 'Notes upon a case of obsessional neurosis', *SE*, 10, pp. 155–249.

Freud, S. 1910, 'The antithetical meaning of primal words', *SE*, 11, pp. 153–162.

Freud, S. 1920a, 'The psychogenesis of a case of homosexuality in a woman', *SE*, 18, pp. 147–170.

Freud, S. 1920b, 'Beyond the pleasure principle, *SE*, 18, pp. 7–64.

Freud, S. 1925, 'Negation', *SE*, 19, pp. 235–240.

Freud, S. 1937, 'Constructions in analysis', *SE*, 23, pp. 257–268.

Freud, S. 1941, 'Letter to Marie Bonaparte (22 August 1938, in)', *Findings, Ideas, Problems, SE*, 23, p. 300.

Freud, S. 1940 [1938], 'An outline of psycho-analysis', *SE*, 23, pp. 139–207.

Geller, P.E. 2000, *International Copyright Law and Practice*, Matthew Bender, New York.

Grosskurth, P. 1986, *Melanie Klein. Her Work and Her World*, Knopf, New York.

Heidegger, M. 1967, *Being and Time* (Eng. trans. by John Macquarrie and Edward Robinson), Blackwell, Oxford.

Ionesco, E. 1951, *The Lesson*, https://collected.jcu.edu/plays/12/

Jakobson, R. 1971, 'Two aspects of language and two types of aphasic disturbances', in R. Jakobson ed., *Fundamentals of Language* (Eng. trans. By Moris Halle), Mouton, The Hague, pp. 69–96.

Janik, A. ed. 1996 [1979], 'Ludwig Wittgenstein, "Letters to Ludwig von Ficker" (Eng. trans. by Bruce Gillette)', in C.G. Luckhardt ed., *Wittgenstein: Sources and Perspectives*, Thoemmes Press, Bristol, pp. 82–98.

King, P.H. and Steiner, R. 1991, *The Freud-Klein Controversies, 1941–1945*, Routledge, London.

Klein, M. 1924, 'The role of the school in the libidinal development of the child', *International Journal of Psychoanalysis*, 5, pp. 312–331.

Kris, E. 1951, 'Ego psychology and interpretation in psychoanalytic therapy', *The Psychoanalytic Quarterly*, 20(1), pp. 15–30.

Kris, E. 1953, 'Ego psychology and interpretation in psychoanalytic therapy', *Yearbook of Psychoanalysis*, 8, pp. 158–171.

Krüger, S. 2011, *Das Unbehagen in der Karikatur. Kunst, Propaganda und persuasive Kommunikation im Theoriewerk Ernst Kris*, Fink, München.

Krüger, S. 2012, 'Fresh brains: Jacques Lacan's critique of Ernst Kris' psychoanalytic method', *American Imago*, 69(4), pp. 507–542.

Lacan, J. 1975 [1933], *De la psychose paranoïaque dans ses rapports avec la personnalité, suivi de Premiers écrits sur la paranoïa*, Seuil, Paris.

Lacan, J. 1976, 'Conférences dans les universités nord-américaines', *Scilicet*, pp. 6–7.

Lacan, J. 2003, *Family Complexes in the Formation of the Individual* (Eng. trans. Cormac Gallagher), Karnac, London.

Laurent, E. 1989, 'Séminaire sur 'La direction de la cure et les principes de son pouvoir'', in AA. VV ed., *Conceptions de la cure en psychanalyse*, The Association Mondiale de Psychanalyse, Buenos Aires (September 1989. Quoted by de Duarte 1997), p. 55.

Leader, D. 1997, *Promises Lovers Make When It Gets Late*, Faber and Faber, London.

Leader, D. 2021, 'Lacan and the Americans', *European Journal of Psychoanalysis* (December 3), Salon, www.journal-psychoanalysis.eu/lacan-and-the-americans/

Little, M. 1951, 'Counter-transference and the patient's response to it', *The International Journal of Psychoanalysis*, 32, pp. 32–40.

Little, M. 1957, 'The analyst's total response to his patient's needs', *International Journal of Psycho-Analysis*, 38, pp. 240–54.

Louette, J.F. 2006, 'Sartre anarchiste, ou démocrate en prose?', *Revue d'histoire littéraire de la France*, 2(106), pp. 285–306.

Luborsky, L. and Singer, B. 1975, 'Comparative studies of psychotherapies: Is it true that everyone has won and all must have prizes?' *Archives of General Psychiatry*, 32.

MacLagan, E. 1923, 'Leonardo in the consulting room', *Burlington Magazine*, 42(238), pp. 54, 57–58.

Marcuse, H. 1955, *Eros and Civilization: A Philosophical Inquiry into Freud*, Beacon Press, Boston.

Martial 2015, *Epigrams* (Eng. trans. Gideon Nisbet), Oxford University Press, Oxford.

Martin, L. 1986, 'Eskimo words for snow: A case study in the general genesis and decay of an anthropological example', *American Anthropologist*, 88, pp. 418–423.

Mitchell, S.A and Margaret Black, M. 1995, *Freud and Beyond: A History of Modern Psychoanalytic Thought*, Basic Books, New York.

Nietzsche, F. 1888, *Twilight of the Idols* (Eng. trans. R.J. Hollingdale), Penguin Classics, London, 1990.

Pinker, S. 1994, *The Language Instinct*, Penguin Books, London.

Pirandello, L. 1921, *Sei personaggi in cerca d'autore* (Eng. trans. *Six Characters in Search of an Author*), Dover Publications, Mineola, 1997.

Porcelli, P. 2004, 'A case of vaginismus (Followed by "Discusssion on 'A Case of Vaginism'")', *Journal of European Psychoanalysis*, 18(I), pp. 112–118, www.journal-psycho-analysis.eu/articles/a-case-of-vaginismus/

Pullum, G.K. 1991, *The Great Eskimo Vocabulary Hoax and Other Irreverent Essays on the Study of Language*, University of Chicago Press, Chicago.

Rachman, A.W. 1998, 'Judicious self-disclosure by the psychoanalyst', *International Forum of Psychoanalysis*, 7, pp. 263–269.

Reich, A. 1951, 'On counter-transference', *International Journal of Psycho-Analysis*, 32, pp. 25–31.

Rose, L. 2007, 'Daumier in Vienna. Ernst Kris, E.H. Gombrich and politics of caricature', *Visual Resources*, 23(1–2), pp. 39–64.

Roudinesco, E. 1986, *La Bataille de cent ans. Histoire de la psychanalyse en France*, vol 2, Seuil, Paris.

Roudinesco, E. 1992, *Jacques Lacan. Esquisse d'une vie, histoire d'un système de pensée*, Fayard, Paris.

Roudinesco, E. and Plon, M. 1997, *Dictionnaire de la psychanalyse*, Fayard, Paris (entry for "Schmideberg Melitta, née Klein"), pp. 949–950.

Sartre, J.P. 1964, *The Words: The Autobiography of Jean-Paul Sartre* (Eng. trans. by Bernard Frechtman and George Braziller), George Braziller, New York.

Schmideberg, M. 1934, 'Intellektuelle hemmung und es-störung', *Internationalen Zeitschrift für Psychoanalyse*, 8.

Schmideberg, M. 1935, 'The mode of operation in psycho-analytic theory, republished as 'the psycho-analysis of asocial children and adolescents'', *The International Journal of Psychoanalysis*, 16, pp. 22–48.

Schreber, D.P. 1903 [2000], *Memoirs of My Nervous Illness*, New York Review of Books, New York.

Siegrist, H. 2004, 'The history and current problems of intellectual property (1600–2000)', in *Axel Zerdick, E-Merging Media. Communication and the Media Economy of the Future*, Springer-Verlag Berlin and Heidelberg GmbH & Co., Heidelberg, pp. 311–329.

Sontag, S. 1978, *Illness as Metaphor*, Farrar Straus Giroux, New York.

Strachey, J. 1934, 'The nature of the therapeutic action of psycho-analysis', *The International Journal of Psychoanalysis*, 15, pp. 127–159.

Swiggers, P. 2014, 'La langue mise en échec(s)', *Recherches sémiotiques*, 34(1–2–3), pp. 59–74. www.erudit.org/en/journals/rssi/2014– v34– n1–2–3– rssi02602/1037146ar/

Turkle, S. 1986, 'Daughters, fighting for Freud's mantle', *The New York Times*, May 18 (Section 7), p. 14.

Winnicott, D.W. 1960, 'Ego distortion in terms of true and false self', in *The Maturational Process and the Facilitating Environment: Studies in the Theory of Emotional Development*, International Universities Press, New York.

Wittgenstein, L. 1922, *Tractatus Logico-Philosophicus*, Kegan Paul, London.

Wittgenstein, L. 2001, *Philosophical Investigations*, Blackwell Publishing, Oxford.

Wortis, J. 1994, *My Analysis with Freud*, Jason Aronson, London.

Young Bruehl, E. 1988, *Anna Freud*, Macmillan, London.

Zafiropoulos, M. 2001, *Lacan et les sciences sociales*, PUF/Humensis, Paris.

Index

For Product Safety Concerns and Information please contact our EU
representative GPSR@taylorandfrancis.com
Taylor & Francis Verlag GmbH, Kaufingerstraße 24, 80331 München, Germany

www.ingramcontent.com/pod-product-compliance
Lightning Source LLC
Chambersburg PA
CBHW050615280326
41932CB00016B/3057

9 781032 482330